A HISTORY OF KEPSTOWE FREIGHT SERVICES LTD.

A HISTORY OF KEPSTOWE FREIGHT SERVICES LTD.

TRUCKING THROUGH THE IRON CURTAIN

MAT IRELAND

PEN & SWORD TRANSPORT

AN IMPRINT OF PEN & SWORD BOOKS LTD.
YORKSHIRE – PHILADELPHIA

First published in Great Britain in 2024 by
Pen and Sword Transport
An imprint of
Pen & Sword Books Ltd.
Yorkshire - Philadelphia

ISBN 978 1 03610 280 7

A CIP catalogue record for this book is available from the British Library.

Typeset in Palatino 11/13 by SJmagic DESIGN SERVICES, India.

Printed and bound by Printworks Global Ltd, London/Hong Kong.

Pen & Sword Books Ltd. incorporates the imprints of Pen & Sword Books: After the Battle, Archaeology, Atlas, Aviation, Battleground, Discovery, Family History, History, Maritime, Military, Politics, Select, Transport, True Crime, Fiction, Frontline Books, Leo Cooper, Praetorian Press, Seaforth Publishing, Wharncliffe and White Owl.

For a complete list of Pen & Sword titles please contact

PEN & SWORD BOOKS LIMITED
George House, Beevor Street, Off Pontefract Road, Hoyle Mill, Barnsley,
South Yorkshire, England, S71 1HN.
E-mail: enquiries@pen-and-sword.co.uk
Website: www.pen-and-sword.co.uk

or

PEN AND SWORD BOOKS
1950 Lawrence Rd, Havertown, PA 19083, USA
E-mail: uspen-and-sword@casematepublishers.com
Website: www.penandswordbooks.com

FSC
www.fsc.org
FSC® C 007031

CONTENTS

FOREWORD

I wrote this in 2022, a time when truck drivers have mobile phones with the internet at their fingertips and a choice of hundreds of different maps. There is satellite navigation, sometimes built into the truck. There is round-the-clock back-up from every major truck manufacturer, as well as tyre companies in every country who can have a fully equipped van at your side within the hour. Automatic gearboxes are standard now, as is air conditioning, a fridge, sometimes even a freezer, and a microwave. You name it, there is a good chance you will find it in the modern truck.

This book covers the 1980s but is mostly set around the early 1990s. Although this is only just over thirty years ago, the leaps in comfort and technology to the present day would seem like something from outer space to the drivers involved here.

The trucks, although mainly modern at the time, had nowhere near as much space inside. The drivers would have needed stacks of paper maps, taking up precious space in the living area. Mobile phones were about, but not only were they hugely expensive, the coverage was nothing like it is today. The roads were bad and that is putting it mildly, and temperatures would range from blistering heat in the summer to bone splintering cold in the winter, which was relentless. On the fabled Middle East trucking routes, the cold was endured but at least you knew you would get some warmth as you got nearer to Arabia. Going to Kazakhstan, you would have to wait to warm up when you finally got back into Europe somewhere. These drivers had to be able to fix any issues themselves on the side of the road, as there was no other choice; that is how life was. Border queues could go on for days with corrupt police and military officials all looking to make a quick dollar out of a 'rich westerner'. You could really question the sanity of anyone who actively chose to plough these trails, year in year out, when a much easier life was available closer to home. Yet the lure of something out of the ordinary was, and still is, too much for some people to resist. No matter what the risks and complications, it was obviously worth setting off to the unknown for an adventurer.

A history such as this is one that is virtually impossible to document completely and accurately. Some people do not wish to participate, some are sadly no longer with us, and with the passing of time, memories can become hazy.

I believe the stories and events in this book are as accurate as we could get. I would like to thank everyone who has taken their time in helping me with this project; everyone named and also the ones whose names do not appear in print. Without you all this would never have got off the ground and to you all I am forever grateful. Long-haul trucking of this nature is what inspired me as a child growing up. Reading magazines showing trucks covered in muck enduring all sorts of problems. Twenty years or so after reading about these journeys, I managed to fulfil my dream and cross the Russian border for the first time in 2007. Although a heck of a lot had changed by then, I was still in ecstasy. The wanderlust bug is still entombed in me, and every week I find myself wondering if a fabled trip to one of these far-flung places may still yet appear for me on the horizon. I hope you enjoy reading this as much as I have piecing it together. The drivers' recollections are as they remember them. There were a lot of other trips undertaken, but they either have not been remembered, or there are no photographs to accompany the tale.

This book is dedicated to the Kepstowe drivers no longer with us to enjoy the nostalgia.

THE FORMATIVE YEARS

Kepstowe Freight services can trace its origins back to 1971. Owner Neil Richardson decided to go it alone after being employed by a company called Freight Shipping International, based at Ludgate Circus in the city of London. Kepstowe was set up, not as a transport company, but as a freight forwarder to the exhibition industry. The cargo would include customers' exhibits (the products that they were looking to display and sell at these fairs), stand fitting materials, and any associated consumable materials such as sales literature, promotional giveaways, food and drink for client entertaining and so on. Potential exhibitors in Russia and Eastern Europe in the 1970s would have little or no experience of a reliable means of shipping to those countries, or the customs procedures on their arrival. Kepstowe's services therefore included consolidating goods in the UK prior to shipment, helping customers prepare and translate customs paperwork into a required language for the country of the exhibition, and arranging the shipment either by road, sea or air to ensure arrival and clearance in time for a show. Following on from the initial export, they would also handle the customs clearance upon arrival, and the unloading, unpacking and delivery of the goods to the customer's stand.

The company would store empty packing materials while the exhibition took place and then reversed all the services as required at the end to return the equipment back home again. Usually in Russia and Eastern Europe this would involve somebody from Kepstowe's UK staff attending the set up and dismantling of the exhibition to deal directly with local

Owner Neil Richardson, taken in Aberdeen at the oil and gas exhibition, trying out a scooter for size. (Lou Johnson)

Right and below: The very early days. With no trucks of their own, Keith Stemp would move containers of equipment for shipment. These photos were taken at the warehouse facilities at Staines. Note the presence of a snail-like logo on the containers. (Lou Johnson)

customs, to liaise with the organisation for providing cranes, forklifts and local labour, and to oversee all the logistics.

Neil established a small office with a very small warehouse in Lavender Hill, south London. With such a small area, getting a truck to load there was exceptionally difficult. The decision was soon made to rent some additional warehouse space in Staines near Heathrow. This was owned by Keith Stemp Transport. Keith and Neil had worked together with previous jobs, so they knew this arrangement would work well for both parties. Neil had recently purchased some 20ft shipping containers that were to be loaded at Staines in preparation for upcoming exhibitions. Keith's trucks would then transport them to the docks for export, usually Purfleet, Tilbury or occasionally Felixstowe.

It didn't take long before a small warehouse was found in Fulham, shared with a company that imported ball bearings from Eastern Europe. This only lasted for a couple of years, however, and in 1982 the company was on the move again, this time to Wandsworth. Here was finally what Kepstowe required, their own integrated warehouse and office space. This became 'home', and it would be so for over a decade.

The first overland trip undertaken with their own trucks was to Moscow in 1979, using a Ford D series and a Mercedes 7.5-tonner. Driven by Neil Richardson and Paul Mew, it was a step into the unknown with regards to them taking their own vehicles. Both trucks were box vans and equipped with tail lifts, something pretty essential with the lack of on-site availability of things like forklift trucks. Proving this was a viable option for the

A busy day at Wandsworth HQ, with several unwashed trucks from the east in for unloading and reloading. (Lou Johnson)

future would steer the fledgling company in the direction of a haulier. Also in the fleet at that time was a Ford Transit, equipped with a 'tilt' body that met GV60 criteria.

This is a load compartment area that complies with regulations for TIR shipments. It can be completely sealed for the reasons of customs. (For example, if it is loaded in London and sealed by customs, as long as that seal is not broken upon its arrival in Moscow, this guarantees the load has not been tampered with.)

Several second-hand trucks and different rental companies later, Volvo Trucks became Kepstowe's choice of vehicle provider. Heathrow Commercials supplied their first purchase of a new tractor unit in 1989, an F10 Globetrotter. The Globetrotter was the biggest cab option available at the time, and it was equipped to give the driver the best possible living space for their time away. Neil believed Volvo trucks were the best to use. He always insisted that every truck was given the highest specification, not just for longevity, but also for driver comfort and load safety. Air suspension on every axle was included in the build, something very rarely optimised in those days. Also fitted was an Arctic Fox diesel heating system. This pumped the truck's hot water from the cooling system through to the diesel tanks to keep them from freezing up, something essential in the middle of a Russian winter. The trucks were equipped with a satellite communication device made by a company called Inmarsat. This consisted of a keyboard and small monitor, from which messages could be sent to and from the truck, comparable to a very basic text message nowadays. This enabled drivers to be reached in the deepest parts of the remotest areas of somewhere like Kazakhstan, something that could be vital if the truck had a major problem and was days away from the nearest settlement. Although this system was never really intended for road transport, it proved its worth time and again for the company.

The Volvo FL6 that was used for local and UK work only. (Lou Johnson)

Lou and Pete Newlyn stopping for lunch in Germany. (Lou Johnson)

Kepstowe fulfilled a pivotal role in the logistics of the biannual Oil and Gas Exhibition in Aberdeen. Sending their staff from London to be on site meant everything ran more smoothly. They arranged the labour and site handling from start to finish, from the arrival of the carpet tiles to the stands being built, and everything being packed away and returned in the back of trucks. At this time, the exhibition was the largest of its kind in the world. It was an ideal place to showcase to prospective customers the level of organisation that they could provide. A lot of their contracts overseas with similar exhibitions would stem from what they witnessed in Aberdeen.

Due to the small number of companies actually exporting to Russia at the time, all purchasing was done through Russia's ministry of foreign trade, which generally specified that the haulage had to be undertaken by a Russian carrier.

This led to a lot of delays in transport, things going missing en route, and so on. Companies began to look at possible alternatives and in the early 1980s contract delivery services were first undertaken alongside the exhibition work.

By virtue of them being in contact with a lot of blue-chip customers through the exhibitions, Kepstowe were asked to provide a general haulage service. A good example of this was Pete Newlyn transporting computers to Moscow on behalf of Redifon. With Pete always accompanying the load, the service was far more reliable, and customers were impressed. The only downside was that they did not have enough trucks and drivers to fulfil all their customers' needs. Martial law was imposed in Poland in 1982, making the overland route almost impossible, so shipping into Finland was the best alternative option. Many loads were subsequently containerised and

On a relatively local job, delivering to Poznan. (Steve Makin)

Taken in scenic Scotland en route to Aberdeen, this VW T25 was used to transport working crew for exhibitions as well as running around the London area to arrange paperwork, etc. (Lou Johnson)

sent to Helsinki port, Finland. This was a far more reliable port than St Petersburg at the time, and accurate delivery date forecasts could still be maintained. The containers were taken onwards to Moscow by Finnish trucks. The Finns already had well-established links with road transport across their border, and their drivers also held multi-entry visas so another issue was already overcome.

As workloads increased, slowly but surely, a small group of reliable British owner-operators and small hauliers established reliable traction work. Kepstowe used a lot of Finnish sub-contractors for unaccompanied trailers into Turku, alongside the stream of containers.

Kepstowe never tried to set up a fully-fledged warehouse and clearance operation of their own in Russia. This would have involved investment with 'trusted' local partners and negotiations with customs for licences. They had very good relations with many sections of Moscow customs built up over years of working at exhibitions and events, but the post-Soviet situation led to a completely new world of goods imported by private organisations, hazy and ever-changing rules, corruption and so on. For those reasons, they opted for agreements with established customs warehouse and clearance operations. Initially, this was with a Finnish–Russian joint venture, JV Sofi – one of the first of this kind – and then when the importance of contact with the importer, briefing drivers, secure parking and information feedback became clear, an office was established at the Octopus warehouse in early 1992. Originally a joint German–Russian venture, this had collapsed leaving the lot vacant. This made goods handling and on-site support for the exhibition work much easier to manage. It was also ideal

Four Finnish sub-contractors awaiting instructions in Moscow. As they have dedicated light boards on the roof, they must have been regular hauliers for them. (Lou Johnson)

for load consolidation and arranging the transport to and from the west. If required, local haulage could be utilised to save delays for their sub-contractors. By now, up to four containers a week of groupage were being shipped from the UK to Moscow via their Finnish container hauliers. (Groupage is a term for a load consisting of multiple items from multiple shippers all transported together in one trailer or container.)

Paul Saunders was transferred from the London office to run the operations out there. He was joined by two local ladies, Marina and Valerie. Eventually they moved to a different location in the city known as MBL sometime in the mid-1990s, but no one can recall the year exactly. This

Lou and a Finnish subbie with one of the many yard dogs on the eternal hunt for some food scraps. (Lou Johnson)

was another customs-approved depot, much the same as the Octopus, however it was a larger site. It was situated on Dubninskaya Ulitsa 83 and would be the last home in Moscow for the company. The site is now a car showroom.

By the late 1990s, it was obvious that they had outgrown their long-established home at Wandsworth. In 1998, a new and larger depot, also with better access for the trucks, was found. It was a little further out of the city at East Moseley. Located at Imber Court Trading Estate, the area, like a lot around the capital city, is now housing, no longer industrial land. This would be the final home for the company.

A quiet day for Lou, Alan King and a Finnish subbie in Moscow. (Lou Johnson)

Paul Saunders with his freshly purchased Ural motorcycle, a bike he still owns to this day. (Steve Tovey)

FROM RUSSIA WITH LOVE

IN THE WAKE OF GLASNOST, KEPSTOWE FREIGHT SERVICES ARE MAKING THE MOST OF 20 YEARS EXPERIENCE RUNNING TO THE SOVIET UNION. STEWART BROWN REPORTS.

One of the great things about experience is that you can use it to make things sound easy. And with 20 years experience of running to the Soviet Union that is precisely what Kepstowe Freight Services' Neil Richardson does.

For Richardson the biggest problem is the Russian winter. It starts in October and stretches through to March with temperatures running at -15°C. Both his vehicles and his drivers have to be equipped to deal with the rigours of cold weather trucking.

In the early days Kepstowe shipped goods through Finland. Now the trucks go straight across Europe. Moscow, one of Kepstowe's regular destinations, is a round trip of 3,700 miles. The South London-based company started as a specialist transporter of equipment to exhibitions and trade fairs. Then when exhibitors started winning orders Richardson found himself being asked to transport the goods they had sold.

Originally the destinations were entirely in the European part of the Soviet Union, to the west of the Urals and the Don, but as the country opens up, so Kepstowe's horizons are widening and their trucks reaching further east. "There were many closed areas where we couldn't go," recalls Richardson, "but that is changing."

While the change has been most rapid in the era of Glasnost, the Soviet Union had in fact started to relax during the period of Brezhnev's rule. But the opening of the Soviet Union's borders has not been without its problems, most noticeably a vast increase in the amount of cross-border traffic which has actually slowed down the process of entering and leaving the Soviet Union rather than speeded it up.

FEBRUARY 32 1992

Left and overleaf pages: A photo from *Trucking International* but due to a printing error, the photo credited to Neil is not the man himself, but someone totally different and not connected to the company at all! Also, the little Mercedes 814 would later be sent to Moscow to work internally for the company there.

The logo depicting a snail stems from a good friend of Neil's who was working for Rank Xerox at the time. He remarked that he thought that the name of the business should be Airscargo, a play on words for the French word for snail, escargot. Neil stuck with Kepstowe; however, he did get a graphic designer to come up with a logo, purely to see what it would look like. He was so impressed he kept it. That logo was only short-lived for use on the trucks themselves. Rob Keir remembers a rather unimpressed Polish police officer. 'He pointed to the logo on the truck and deemed it inappropriate as he had stopped me for speeding.'

The Kepstow fleet comprises five Volvo F10s and F12s and an 814 Mercedes. One of the F10s is a 4x2 which pulls a drawbar trailer; the others are artics including the company's newest — a 6x2 left-hand-drive F12 with the appropriate registration H1 KGB.

Neil Richardson doesn't believe in half measures on specification or servicing. The Volvos have fuel line heaters, engine block heaters and, of course, cab heaters. They are also air suspended, which Richardson argues is kinder to the truck, the driver and the load. "There's no doubt about it — air ride is excellent. The goods travel better and we get much less damage."

The Volvos are serviced by Kepstowe's local dealer and Richardson has clear views on the importance of keeping on top of servicing. "It's better to replace or repair something before it fails," he argues — and few long-distance operators would disagree.

The choice of Volvos was dictated quite simply by driver preference. "That's what the drivers wanted and that's what we've bought." The trucks don't do exceptionally high mileages during their four or five years in the Kepstowe fleet because during the summer months they spend time on runs to other Eastern European countries, often on specialist exhibition work with low average daily mileages. Consequently at the end of four years they may not have covered more than 400,000 km.

Richardson is satisfied with the Volvos' overall performance although he has had some delays when Volvo agents in Budapest and Hanover have taken a few days to source parts. And he's fairly relaxed about getting help in the Soviet Union. The last few years have seen fleets of Volvos and Mercedes trucks arrive in major Soviet cities and this means that in the event of a problem there should be assistance at hand.

Diesel availability has never presented a problem behind the Iron Curtain. Its poor cold performance means that

it's not a popular choice for Soviet vehicles, and queues at filling stations are therefore invariably for petrol. The problem facing Kepstowe's drivers is that the storage facilities at fuelling sites in Russia and its neighbouring states ›››

Above: Neil Richardson, an old hand at running to the Soviet Union.
Below: Kepstowe use hardy drivers prepared to cope with unfriendly weather conditions.

Trucking (33) **International**

Above: Driver's vehicles need to be deemed reliable enough to make the arduous journey. Below: Kepstowe Freight on the road to Minsk.

are often primitive and that the fuel is waxing before it is transferred to the truck's tank. With the on-board heating facilities which Kepstowe specifies, the diesel is actually being kept in better conditions on the truck than at the fuelling sites. Blocked fuel filters are a source of winter problems.

"Running to Russia is a hard business," says Richardson, and he speaks from the experience of having done it himself. Although the company started as a specialist transporter, it now carries all types of goods and having Russian-speaking staff helps smooth the operation and secure return loads. But a round trip to Moscow is still likely to involve the driver being away for ten or eleven days.

"It suits a certain type of driver and we do all we can to support him if he has a breakdown." Richardson chooses his drivers — and the owner-drivers who work for him — with care. Apart from using owner-drivers who seem likely to find the long hauls to Russia appealing, he uses those with a vehicle "you can reasonably expect will make the journey". The oldest truck in the Kepstowe fleet is E-registered.

The drawbar F10 is the odd-man-out in the Kepstowe operation and Richardson is not convinced that he'll replace it with another. An artic tractor is more likely to be his choice. "With 13.5m trailers there's not going to be that much advantage for us in running a drawbar — and it is more expensive to run than an artic.

"There also has to be a relationship between the cost of a vehicle and the conditions of the roads it runs over."

The truck must not be too sophisticated and on some Soviet roads we find the drawbar trailer too low with things like brake actuators getting knocked off."

With 20 years experience in Soviet trucking Neil Richardson is well placed to benefit from the changes currently taking place in the rapidly-changing ex-communist states. His concern now must not be so much about fulfilling a transport challenge but about the implications of the wider economic changes and their bearing on all aspects of east-west trade. **MTI**

THE STAFF

Lou Johnson

Lou had grown up knowing Neil Richardson as a friend and also work colleague from around the age of eighteen. Lou's stepfather, Keith Stemp, was the first haulier for Kepstowe when they started transporting various goods using shipping containers.

Although he holds a C&E licence, Lou was usually found driving the small Mercedes rigid truck. This involved a lot of smaller work in specialised areas of haulage like theatre tours.

Lou seldom saw any of the other drivers, except when passing on the roads. Being involved pretty much from the get-go on a self-employed basis, Lou was to be the second-longest serving driver at Kepstowe. Lou's wife would also drive the Transit van on occasions when the workload was heavy.

Robert Keir

Robert joined the company at the beginning of 1980. Although employed as an office-based member of staff, his first trip was to Moscow in the February of that year along with Paul Mew in the aforementioned trucks.

Beth King

Beth King joined the team at Kepstowe in 1994. Answering an advertisement in the London University Press, she met Rob Keir for the first time when he interviewed her.

'I studied French and Russian at university. I was fascinated with Russia, the Soviet Union as it was originally. Having grown up with the Cold War at its height, and with every single villain on things like James Bond being a Russian, I thought this was a bit unfair. I just wanted to know more about this mysterious country, from the revolution through the twentieth century and why it became such an enigma. To study the language, you really need to be taught it, unlike a language say like Italian which you can self-teach. I spent six months in Voronezh studying in my third year to really get a feel of the country and a good grip on the language.

'My role at Kepstowe would involve a lot of on-site work for the exhibitions and conferences, which really appealed to me. I did not want to be office-bound, the opportunity to explore these countries while getting paid for it I guess is much the same reason why a lot of people become truck drivers. Eventually the job did take me all over, from Moscow to Almaty and beyond, it was fantastic.'

Matt and Pat Towse

The New Zealand-born brothers, Matt and Pat, both found employment with Kepstowe by responding to an advertisement in the NZ news UK, a weekly newspaper aimed at expat New Zealanders in the UK.

Pat was allocated the company's Volvo F10 Globetrotter when it was first purchased. After a couple of years behind the wheel, he came off the road to work in the office.

Matt was taken on as a non-HGV driver initially, driving one of the several smaller vehicles. After two years they paid for him to take his full articulated licence. After a few years of driving, Matt changed roles and started working in the office in London. Before long, he was transport manager and spent four years in this role.

'At its height, alongside our own equipment and sub-contractors, we were renting in 120 trailers from Central Trailer Rentco and Transamerica Leasing to cover the volume of work we had.

Matt Towse, on the left, at the oil and gas exhibition, Aberdeen. On his right is Henry Osbourne, Kepstowe's exhibitions manager. (Lou Johnson)

I was then transferred to Baku when they set up an office there. This was mainly to handle the annual oil and gas exhibition which was a large and regular job. But there was also a lot of other work from this area, internally and also exporting. I was covering the whole of the region, not just Azerbaijan.'

Dave Button

Dave: 'If I had not have been having such a bad run in Turkey, I probably would never have started!' laughs Dave about joining the firm.

Running to the Middle East with a 'seller' (a loaded truck and trailer; you unload the cargo, sell the truck and trailer at the destination, and fly home. Once quite a common practice.), Dave was halfway up the Tarsus mountains, with the engine in bits on the floor.

'I phoned home and got a message asking me to ring this guy who was offering me some work. This particular trip was just one of them where everything had gone wrong, and frankly I was just fed up with the whole lot. I think we all have days like that!'

When the truck was repaired, Dave eventually got to the Arabian peninsula, flew home and returned the call.

'I was initially offered three months' work for one particular contract they had, starting in September of 1994. My name had been put forward by a couple of people as someone who may be interested in the work. That last trip being so bad, I thought to myself "why not", and so I took a chance. The three months turned into seven years in the end.'

Steve Makin

Steve's first trip to Russia was for Cheltenham-based Ralph Davis. 'I was getting a bit fed up with constantly running to Spain and back, and then all of a sudden, I was given a trip to Moscow. I believe I was the first of Ralph's trucks to go to Russia, this was around 1989.'

Generally going to St Petersburg, although sometimes to Moscow as well, Steve kept running there until he managed to get a job with owner-operator Chris Everitt.

'I wanted to work for Kepstowe, but as they did not have any jobs going I worked for Chris first. Coming back from Ukraine once, I can't remember exactly where, all I had in the way of tyres when I had a blowout was a trailer super single. Of course, you couldn't just phone up a tyre company and get a van out like you can these days, it was either fit it or try and find a tyre myself! The wheel fitted, so in my eyes it was plenty good enough! It got me back to the UK. When a job came up working for Kepstowe direct, I left Chris, and I began working there directly.'

When Steve Makin started with Chris Everitt, he was in Ukraine and out of spare tyres for the steer axle, so he had to resort to using a trailer super single to get him going again. (Steve Makin)

Michael Packham

Mickey joined from a company called Pro-Motor, who also specialised in long-haul trucking at the time. His first trip was in 1988 for Pro-Motor, giving him a glimpse of work in the east. 'I was taking some camera equipment out to Moscow for the Gorbachev–Reagan summit they were holding. This was during the communist era and my first taste of life behind the Iron Curtain. There were three of us together. Myself and one other had ITN's news equipment, and the third had some JCB machinery that was exhibited at the Kremlin and was being bought by the government. We felt like we were being watched every minute of the day. It was enjoyable as it was something so different to life at home.'

Having left Pro-Motor, he then went to work for another Russian transport company called Barry Martin Transport, mostly running between their depot in Crawley and Moscow. While doing this work he became friendly with a lot of the Kepstowe regulars on the route.

'I was told there was likely a driving job coming up, and it was when Pat Towse came off the road there was a vacancy, and so I got myself the job there and then. What I really loved about the job was the camaraderie. Not only among us at Kepstowe, but with the other handful of Brits on the trail east, along with the Dutch, French and Germans. We would all inevitably meet up at the same watering holes, and no one would go past you if you were stopped, even if you did not need help.

'Most of the work I did was to the Moscow depot, but the occasional trip beyond, like Samara for Pepsi. I also went to Almaty in Kazakhstan for the oil and gas exhibition, as well as Baku several times for the same reason. I even flew out there to do some site work, unloading trucks and the like. It certainly made a difference flying in and back home, I have never turned a trip around so quick.

Nick Reynolds, left, about to be hoisted by Mickey Packham. (Mickey Packham)

When the Rouble collapsed in 1998 with the so-called Russian flu, I knew that the best was well and truly over, and the writing was on the wall, so I managed to find a job completely out of driving for once, helping out a friend labouring on building sites. I eventually returned behind the wheel, but I only ever went as far east as the Czech Republic. Even that country was a world apart from how I had previously seen it in a truck when it was Czechoslovakia while I was working for Pro-Motor.'

John Mantle

John was another to come from Pro-Motor like Mick. Having undertaken his first trip to Moscow in 1984, he brought with him a wealth of knowledge about the routes and borders. Starting in 1989 after being made redundant, he was the third driver on the books. His first truck was a rental tractor unit until they started to buy their own.

Vince Coventon

Vince was an example of 'it's not what you know, but who', though he did have one ace up his sleeve.

'One day I was looking around the local WH Smith, and in their bargain bucket they had a Russian language double cassette and book pack, reduced to 99p. As I have always liked languages, I bought it and began listening. Perhaps it was a premonition. About three months after this chance purchase, I was providing some holiday cover for an owner-driver friend of mine and was sent to Kodak at Watford to load a trailer to take to Belgium. When I arrived and booked in, I went into the driver's room and bumped into Richard Warren. I had worked with him several years previous at a company called Young Brothers. We got chatting, as drivers do, and I asked him where he was going. When he told me Moscow, I thought he was pulling my leg. But he pulled out his

L–R: Unknown, John Mantle, Les Rivett, who worked for Peter Gilder and was sub-contracted in for the trip, Finnish driver, Chris Everitt and 'Turks', who was a stand builder for MEMS, one of Kepstowe's customers. Taking a coffee break in Baku. (Mickey Packham)

collection information and a big bundle of Rouble notes, and I knew he was serious. I told him that I fancied a job doing that sort of thing, and he said he would have a word with the office when he next spoke to them.

'Not long after, I happened to be passing their depot, so thought I would pop in and see if I could get myself a job. I sat with Rob Keir, and I could tell the ad hoc interview was not going quite how I had hoped, due to the fact that they had recently been inundated with applications after a magazine feature. I thought I would let them know that I could speak Russian, and this caught his attention. Although I was far from fluent, I was confident I could get by, and more importantly get myself understood and through things like customs. He offered me a trip they had coming up. I took it on, and from there I spent four years working for them. It was busier in the summertime, which suited me as the winters are certainly challenging, and I was happy to let others who were more money hungry take that work. That said, I still did quite a few wintertime trips, but not back-to-back like others would. When my twin sons were born, I left on good terms because I wanted to spend time with them growing up, but with the option of returning again sometime in the future. Sadly, this never came to fruition.'

Steve Tovey

Steve started around the same time as Dave Button and Steve Makin.

'I was also on the same initial three-month contract as the others. There were no spare tractor units at the time, so the three of us had rental low-cabbed Volvo FHs. I finished later in 1999, my father's health was deteriorating and so I had handed my notice in just before they had to start laying drivers off. I went to work for Richard at Fleetwood's but doing UK-only work.'

Steve Tovey and his Volvo FH. (Steve Tovey)

SUB-CONTRACTORS – THE BACKBONE OF HAULAGE

Within such a niche market, owning and operating your own vehicles was a very costly exercise. The advantages were that you had a company employee on site for the duration of any exhibition that could help with your customer's needs, and certainly in the early days, office staff would double as a driver to perform such a role. But when there was downtime, a truck parked up for weeks, perhaps months at a time was essentially a money pit. This was why they decided to rely more on sub-contractors for their work. They could drop off as soon as the work was quiet and come back in as required. There will be some names that appear in this book but they do not have their own segment here. This is because they perhaps only did one or two jobs, in between their own international work.

The Braintree Satellite Yard

Cordons Farm is located in the sleepy village of Cressing just outside Braintree in Essex. It had already proved to be a hub of international haulage. M&C Transport, well known for their Middle East haulage, had been based there before they closed their doors in the late 1980s, and so trucks had already travelled to weird and wonderful places from this starting point with all sorts of cargo, from the normal to the bizarre.

From this unassuming yard, a dedicated plethora of truckers would call it home to their trucks and operations. These were Alan Johnson, Steve Clark, Alan King and Dave Kane, 'Fast' Fred Phillips, Chris Everitt, David Jamieson and Alan Bremner. Alan Johnson and Steve Clark had both previously been employed as drivers with M&C. Alongside these was also a small commercial repair and maintenance garage called Greyhound Commercials. This was run by Steve Gray and Paul 'Rab' Jose. Steve had worked in M&C's workshop, and when they ceased trading he started his company without having to move very far. Rab himself did a few trips to Russia to cover Steve Clark's truck. This small company generally looked after the aforementioned drivers and companies' trucks, something that kept them very busy when they arrived back from the East.

Alan Johnson

Alan was Kepstowe's first regular sub-contractor. His usual work plying the fabled Middle East trucking routes had gone a bit quiet, and so he had picked up some more local work for a company called Ferryline Forwarding from Kent. This involved delivering Ford engines from their South Wales plant to Saarlouis in Germany. Alan came to start working for Kepstowe after a chance conversation one day with Pat Towse in Zeebrugge docks while on this interlude for Ferryline. Pat remembered Alan instantly as he had been helped by him in Istanbul a few years previously while working elsewhere, and they had kept in touch on the road ever since. Pat was double manning a truck with Pete Newlyn at the time.

'We are off to Leningrad!' Pat exclaimed to Alan. This really piqued his interest as it was somewhere that Alan fancied going to. Pat told him that he would have a word with the powers that be in the office as

Alan Johnson cooking up some 'camion stew' on the truck's catwalk. To his left is Steve Makin. (Alan Johnson)

they seemed to be expanding and could use some reliable sub-contractors.

'You often hear comments like that, which usually lead to nothing, but sure enough I received a call asking me to pop in if I was passing for a chat. So the next time I was passing Wandsworth I called in to do just that. We all got on well, and sure enough they offered me a trip to Russia to see how we would get on with each other. My first job was in 1989, with a step frame tilt taking equipment for a large accountancy firm who were opening up an office in Moscow.'

Alan would become influential in the recruitment of future sub-contractors, and most would be working via him rather than directly. Aware that his reputation would be on the line, he was careful about who he put forward. He knew the pitfalls and how specialised the jobs could be, meaning that anyone joining had to be reliable and hard working.

Steve Clark

Steve Clark is an example of 'it's not what you know but who', which is often the case in the haulage industry. Working with Alan Johnson on and off for several years would lead to him being one of the first owner-drivers on board. 'I had known Alan since our days working for UKON Trucking together, who had long since ceased trading. When I heard about this work he was doing for Kepstowe I was certainly interested in giving it a go. We were operating out of the same transport yard at the time, so it seemed like a natural progression.

'I had a Volvo F12 initially, which I then traded in against a Daf 95. Both of them were good trucks, but they lacked space, as most trucks at the time did. When I sold the Daf I bought a Renault Magnum, which was a world apart for living in, no more getting dressed laying down on the bunk!'

Steve Clark sheltering from the rain en route to Baku. (Steve Clark)

After Steve had his Volvo resprayed, it was immediately nicknamed the fire truck for obvious reasons! Seen parked here with Nick Reynolds in Finland en route to the Russian border. (Steve Clark)

Freddie Phillips

Fred was another small haulier, with three trucks. He had dabbled with international work on and off, and being in the same yard as Alan, naturally they were friends and often talked work.

'I had my trucks doing Italian work at the time and thought I would give it a go. The rates for the work seemed pretty good, so why not? Initially I only put one truck on hire to them, but as that proved a success I then had all three pulling Kepstowe trailers. My driver Mick Ashby was the first on the work, and lasted the longest on there. I did a bit myself, and enjoyed the work. I mostly only drive to Moscow, with just a few trips further afield. One job took me a fair way further east, but sadly I cannot remember where exactly this was. All of my trucks were Volvos, which were second hand, and as they got worn out on this work they got replaced by newer Volvos. They were good trucks and well suited to the work and held themselves together better than most in my experience.'

Michael Ashby

Mick worked for Fred Phillips, starting late in 1994 with a trip to Moscow.

'I enjoyed it because no two trips were ever the same. You just never knew exactly what was going to happen,' recalls Mick. Mick mostly travelled to Ukraine and

L–R: Dave Button, Mike Ashby, Gordon Jones, Richard Warren, Steve Tovey. (Steve Tovey)

Moscow, with the occasional trip further east, but not to any of the other Russian states. Mick passed away on 10 May 2022.

Thomas Alan King and Dave Kane

Thomas King, known to everyone by his middle name Alan, and Dave Kane were two owner-operators who had developed a business partnership to help create a bit of strength and security instead of being totally on their own. Alan was certain he would not be heading east in his career, being quite happy staying somewhat more local.

'I remember being in the yard, and Nice (Nigel Harness) was talking about a trip he had just done, how many days he had sat at this border, and then that border. And I thought to myself, "Sod that, you won't get me doing that sort of nonsense." Well, look how that turned out,' he says with a laugh.

Alan was engaged on UK distribution work at the time. He had been to Germany once before but no further. However, after discussing the rates the jobs were paying with various others, he decided to give it a go. Starting for Kepstowe in 1994, initially he was just loading and unloading trailers in the UK, before being asked if he would like a trip to Poznan in Poland in January. There was a part-loaded fridge trailer, loaded with Chubb safes, at Kepstowe's depot. Alan then took this trailer to Dordrect in the Netherlands and then to Koln in Germany to complete the loading before heading to the German–Polish border at Szczecin. It was about three minutes past midnight and his birthday. Waiting to drive through the gate to start customs with a bright spotlight being shone in his face, he thought to himself 'What the hell am I doing this for?' Once he was through it was much more plain sailing to get to Poznan and unloaded. Once empty he ran back into Germany and parked at Recklinghausen for the weekend. The start of the new

Alan beside his second MAN queueing at Brest. (Alan King)

Alan's third MAN he ran. He found them to be very reliable on the runs east. (Alan King)

week saw him drive into Belgium and load chocolates for Marks and Spencer's in England.

His first trip into Russia started easily enough. Alan was running with Chris Everitt and Steve Makin en route to Moscow. 'The only problem with Chris is that he drives off like a scalded cat, so I had to make sure I kept up with him to get to Moscow! As it was February the weather was not exactly ideal, there was plenty of snow and ice about to keep me on my toes,' Alan laughs.

After unloading in Moscow, he was sent for a return load of sheepskins from Gomel, which is now part of Belarus. 'If you have never had the so-called pleasure of transporting skins, you don't know what you are missing. Blood, muck and smell, a truly horrible job, but I presume it pays well! With those horrible items safely enclosed in the fridge, it was time to head home. When I arrived back in the UK, customs wanted to have a look inside the trailer. I told the dog handler that she really doesn't want to look in the back, but she was insistent. So I cracked the doors and pulled them open, and the smell that rolled out soon changed her mind. I was instructed to get the doors closed as quick as I could and get out of their compound.'

Chris Everitt

Chris was another owner-operator and at the time he was operating two trucks. Having previously worked for an abnormal load specialist haulier named Vanguard based in London, he had already undertaken a couple of Russian trips on their behalf so he knew the ropes.

There was a long-running joke among the other drivers about what time Chris would start. 'I would always work on local time, whereas others would stick with British time. For me, unlike the employed drivers, time was money.

The quicker I got the job done, the more money I would potentially make. I would rather start fairly early in the morning and park up long before dark. It was a bit of an unwritten rule that you don't drive at night in Russia. The roads and driving standards made it perilous within daylight hours, let alone after dark when a lot of people had been having a cheeky tipple of vodka! With the time difference, if I was thinking of starting at 6am local, this could well be 3am GMT, something that didn't sit too well with the boys who liked to have a few beers at the end of the day.'

Chris was a fan of the Iveco brand, initially starting sub-contracting with a 190.36 Turbostar. Steve Makin was subsequently employed to drive this. Chris purchased a second one to drive himself, a 190.42, however, this one was damaged in an accident. The pair were part exchanged for a brand new Iveco Eurostar from their main dealership in Bedford. This would be built to Chris's specification with the work in mind.

'I wanted it to be left-hand drive, for the obvious reason that the UK is the only place right-hand drive is any good. The middle axle was a pusher type. This means that it does not steer but it can be lifted when you are empty to save tyre wear. The main reason for any British company to get a truck that is 6 × 2 is for a saving on the vehicle's annual revenue.

'I had it adapted so even when the truck was loaded I could lift it to gain traction when it was winter time by having an override switch. A secondary night heater was fitted inside the cab, but rather than run off the truck's diesel like the factory one, this was petrol powered, with its own small tank on the rear of the truck. As petrol freezes at a lot lower temperature than diesel, it meant that if the main heater packed up I could still stay warm. A second fuel tank was also specified to make the most of the extremely cheap diesel you could buy on the road in Russia. The fuel lines were all insulated for the harsh winters with heaters fitted in line to stop any freezing up.

'Because I had done the work with Vanguard, they used to get me to do more of the heavier stuff if Alan Johnson could not cover it. I didn't mind too much because it meant you did not have to try and strip a tilt trailer down in winter to unload it. The downside was that the loads would often be heavier or out of gauge so if this was in Europe it could mean waiting for permits and escorts, something which could cost you time. There was a difference in the rates to compensate for these sort of things.'

Fleetwood Transport

Fleetwood Transport take their name from the slightly more famous band of the same name, Fleetwood Mac. Nick Reynolds was the original owner and he was married to the band manager's ex-wife. The company was trading as Fleetwood Mobile Studios. The original operation purely had a mobile recording studio and was not involved in road transport at all. Initially, this studio was mounted on the chassis of a D-series Ford truck, but as soon as Nick got the right offer of a Ford Transcontinental that he'd had his eye on, the D series was replaced. Nick undertook almost all of the work himself to switch the body to the Transcontinental.

Nick's first trip to Russia in the aforementioned Transcontinental was in 1984. On 7 January he found himself at Helmstadt, the former East German frontier.

'I was sat there, freezing cold, having guns pointed at me by miserable-looking border guards, and I thought to myself I must be stark raving bonkers to be doing this! Anyway, eventually I managed to get the truck through and to the Russian border. I also had my wife with me at the time. We managed to arrange visas eventually, this was all a steep learning curve for us at the time. Eventually we got to Moscow and got ourselves back home again. After that trip, we heard about Kepstowe and approached them to help with the paperwork and visa side of things. At the time, all documentation

The only photo of the entire Fleetwood fleet together at the same time! Taken in Helsinki docks. (Rod Withers)

Parked at the Riders Motel, this is the Fleetwood Scania complete with mobile recording studio. (Steve Makin)

needed translating, and Kepstowe were the only transport company in a position to arrange this for us.' This would prove to be the start of a long and fruitful working relationship. The studio would travel regularly to Russia for things such as the Bolshoi Ballet and other live concerts.

Eventually as the workload increased for the company, a second-hand articulated trailer with a studio was purchased, along with a Scania 112 tag axle tractor unit to pull it to wherever it was required. At the time, Kepstowe were getting busier and busier with their overland service, and they kept asking if Fleetwood would send their Scania tractor unit with one of their own trailers to Russia when their studio work was slack. Because of the possibility of losing a potential booking, Nick was reluctant to send his only truck. As the question got asked more and more, Nick spoke with Richard Warren, who was employed by the Kent firm Dockspeed at the time. Richard was doing European haulage with the odd trip a little further east at the time. Nick proposed buying a second tractor unit and sub-contracting this one to Kepstowe to help with their work demands. Richard agreed and another second-hand Scania 113 was sourced, and he found himself as Fleetwood's first driver.

On his first trip to Russia, Richard met up with a former owner-driver called Michael Mudie. Michael was heading back west and met Richard in the customs compound at the German-Polish border at Frankfurt Oder. Kepstowe had asked Michael to keep an eye out for Richard as he was on his first trip. Michael informed Richard that there were also a couple of other Kepstowe drivers in front of him. As he continued eastbound, and once past Warsaw, Richard found he was in unknown territory. He made his way to Brest, and the border with Russia. This is now Belarus, but at the time, regarding customs, there was no further border with Russia itself. Here he met with another sub-contractor, who showed him just how not to do the job! Taking an extremely leisurely pace towards Moscow, he stopped at just about every Intourist hotel and parking area. At the time, there were no other real facilities for drivers to stop at. The route from the border is approximately 1,200km, but they stopped for the night firstly at Brest, Minsk, then Smolensk, before finally getting to Moscow. Upon arrival, they met up with a man called Paul Saunders from the Kepstowe office, who promptly gave them a severe dressing down for taking so much time. The loads they had on were for a regular customer called Contracts Abroad. This company would ship out everything needed to build any western company's new office buildings due to a lack of such basic materials in Russia. The loads would see the building project right through. The initial loads would be basics like bricks and plasterboard, and loads would continue heading out until the office furniture arrived and the new building was open for business. With his first load delivered, Richard headed east to Kazan to reload flat-pack furniture back to England.

Rod Withers

One man's loss is another man's gain, well that's certainly how Rod ended up with his job at Fleetwood.

'At the time I was doing your more usual European driving, a lot out to Spain, Italy and so on. A work colleague of mine at the time told me he had been for an interview with Fleetwood but did not get offered the job as he lacked any left-hand drive experience. I had driven left-hand drive trucks before when I was in the army, and he had mentioned to me that they went to places like Russia, which certainly appealed to me as I had always wanted to go that bit further afield. I obtained their phone number from my somewhat deflated colleague and gave them a shout. I was invited up for an interview by Nick Reynolds, and while I was there, I did a test drive in the truck that would become mine if I was offered the job. I managed not to hit anything, and so Nick said it was

Rod Withers on the M/V *Garden* en route to Turku, Finland. (Rod Withers)

mine. I gave my two weeks' notice to my employer and then my first job turned into a real rush one. I was asked if I could go to Poland and do a trailer change. This was right before Christmas and my wife had already put her foot down and told me that I have to be home for Christmas. So I hot-footed it east, and managed to ship back into Dover on Christmas Eve!'

Rod started work right at the tail end of 1993. His first trip to Russia was a bit of an eye-opener.

'I followed Steve Clark to Moscow, and the best bit of advice he gave me was to never go with an agent at night if they come knocking on your door outside of office hours. I was left parked at a truck park on the ring road around Moscow, as Steve was destined elsewhere. Sure enough, in the middle of the night, someone knocks on the cab door. I pull back the cab's curtains, and standing there is a man claiming he is my customs agent. I told him to give me his card and come back in the morning. One hour later and he was back, insisting that I must go with him. I point-blank refused and once again told him to come back in the morning. When I got up, I went and found a phone box and called Kepstowe's Moscow office to report the incident. When I did, all hell broke loose! As Steve had predicted, the mysterious man was not their agent by a long stretch. Twenty minutes later the real agent came to meet me and took me to offload the Kodak equipment I had on. I was really glad Steve had imparted that pearl of wisdom before we went. Not long after this had happened to me, I learnt that another British driver had not been so lucky. He fell for the scam, went with this 'agent' and ended up being held up at gunpoint somewhere around Moscow. The entire load he was carrying was stolen, and he was found tied up in his cab.

Rod enjoyed the job greatly, the variety in loads and destinations meant that no two weeks were ever the same. Eventually, pressure from home forced his hand into tending his resignation. 'I loved it, working for Fleetwood was one of the best times of my life. I would certainly do it all over again given the chance.'

Danny McAuliffe

Hailing from Zambia, Danny came to Europe looking for adventure and travel. After becoming friends with Chris Everitt, he ended up doing approximately two years sub-contracting through Alan Johnson before working directly for Kepstowe, mostly moving out of gauge loads. Danny's memory of his time at Kepstowe sadly is very hazy. However, initially he was running a 6 × 4 Foden truck, something that was certainly unusual at the time. A trip to Kazakhstan was undertaken in a winter and he has supplied a couple of photographs. He now resides in Cornwall as a farmer.

Alan Douglas

Alan was another well-known face in this ultra-long-haulage family. He had previously sub-contracted work for Astran, engaged on Middle East trucking, before moving onto newer uncharted routes, so he knew a few of the old hands. 'I had finished the Middle East and I had undertaken four trips to a gold mine in Zarafshan, Uzbekistan, for another company called Eurogate. Initially I had an old Ford Transcontinental, which I then traded in against a Volvo F16. This was new to Matthews Transport in Great Yarmouth, and I was given the deal by Duffield's Volvo dealer Neil Jarrold. It turned out to be one hell of a truck, strong as an ox and it could pull a house down. They were known to be heavy on fuel, but with the cost of diesel beyond Europe, this really was not an issue for me. What it cost me more for in diesel I gained on the knackered old roads out east.

'Doing this run, I had crossed paths with a few of the Kepstowe drivers as well. At the time this work came about, I was at home and I phoned my good friend Roly Long for a chinwag. He mentioned an upcoming run for Kepstowe going to Baku, and they were possibly looking for another two sub-contractors. Our names duly made their way to Neil Richardson's desk and he called us both up for a chat.

Alan Douglas behind the wheel of his Volvo F16. (Mickey Packham)

One advantage I held was that I was a mechanic by trade and could keep older things going if required. It turned out the forklift that they had on site in Baku was a little past its prime, but he asked if I could keep it running. I agreed, and with that Roly and I were on board for this trip. After my first exhibition, Neil asked if I would come on board full time, as it turned out mainly to help keep the forklift going!'

Ian Mellor

Ian was an owner-driver undertaking long-distance and Middle Eastern trucking in a Foden. Coming on board at the right time, he fell into the work easily enough through his long-term friend and employee Dave Button. They had first met back in the late 1980s, when Dave had taken him on his first overland trips to Turkey and Qatar. Since then, they had stayed in touch. However, Ian didn't actually use his own truck for traction, but was a sub-contracting driver initially before a full-time job on the books came about. Ian passed away on 2 July 2022.

'Nice' Nigel Harness

Nice only undertook a few trips for Kepstowe. He was a well accomplished and experienced long-distance haulier in his own right, however, and operating from the same Braintree yard as the others meant he was a well-known face. At the time he was mostly involved in transport to Russia and beyond, but for a rival company. However, with the nature of the

Ian Mellor posing with his Russian fur hat, bought from a local vendor. (Dave Button)

Finnish driver Mikko Vepsäläinen with a trailer loaded for Baku, which he only took as far as Moscow. (Mikko Vepsäläinen)

transport, they would often meet up on the roads somewhere along the trail.

Finnish Sub-contractors

I have tried my best to locate anyone from Finland who worked on Kepstowe's behalf, but it was a difficult task.
One Finnish driver I found is Mikko Vepsäläinen. He was working for a man called Juha Kaipainen, who owned a small haulage company. In 1994, Mikko made his first Russian trip for Kepstowe to Moscow. Most of the work he did would take him to the country's capital, however he did undertake one trip that took him north-east to the town of Pereslavl-Zalessky, with a consignment of photographic material for long-standing customer Kodak. The work for Kepstowe lasted until 1999 for Mikko, and since finishing he has not been back there in a truck.

IN MEMORY OF ...

Sadly a few of the former drivers had passed away before this book was written. They are gone, but certainly not forgotten.

Peter Newlyn

Pete was the first driver employed by Kepstowe. He had previously worked for Keith Stemp, who provided Kepstowe Transport before they purchased their own trucks. He was 'loaned' to Kepstowe initially by Keith when they were looking for a driver. Neil then asked if he could take him on officially full time instead of him returning to Keith. Fortunately, he agreed, something that these days would certainly be a rare occurrence! A DAF rigid and drawbar trailer was purchased in the spring of 1980, and the keys given to Pete. Not only was he the first driver on the books, but he also went on to become the longest serving, until the close of the company. Pete passed away in 2015.

Gordon Jones

'If there was a souvenir shop selling tat, that is where you would find Gordon,' Richard Warren laughs. Gordon was one of life's eccentrics, and this was something much needed on work like this. Nick Reynolds remembers once pulling up alongside him in the middle of nowhere in

Below left: Peter Newlyn in Baku. (Mickey Packham)

Below right: Gordon Jones striking a pose in Baku. (Mickey Packham)

Russia. He rolled his window down, and said with a feigned plum in his mouth, 'Well old boy, I think it is time for a nice gin and tonic, what do you think?'

Gordon was another driver who had made the switch across from Promotor Transport like Mickey Packham and John Mantle. He had also worked for another Russian specialist, Barry Martin Transport; however, this work had not taken him further than Moscow so the work once again became an adventure for him.

Michael Mudie

'The most unlikely truck driver you ever met,' Alan Douglas remembers fondly. 'He looked more like a bank manager or accountant than a trucker.'

Michael was another owner-driver. He had been working for another long-gone company called Felgate Services from Essex doing European work. He undertook a couple of trips for Kepstowe working through David Croome, although these were not actually to Russia. Owner Neil Richardson spotted something in him as a potential haulier on their behalf, and so he asked Alan Johnson if he could sub-contract through him, to which Alan obliged. After a few incidents and various issues, running his own truck was proving to be quite a strain. When Kepstowe offered him a job directly with them, he gladly accepted. This eased the burden on him and Michael took everything in his stride and was seldom seen to lose his temper. He had an extremely dry sense of humour. 'Miles make smiles' was one of his favourite sayings. He was quite a keen reader, and would often take books with him from his local library in Braintree. With a time limit on their return, he would often phone the workers there to renew his books over the phone. The ladies would often look forward to his calls from these far-flung places.

'One thing he was famous for was his sister's cakes, which she would bake

Michael Mudie. (Mickey Packham)

for him every trip. I have never known anyone to slice a cake so thin, they would be about as thick as a Rizla cigarette paper to make the cake last as long as possible. He would always want the napkin or piece of tin foil back to reuse the next day,' Richard Warren remembers fondly.

Alan Bremner

Alan was a larger-than-life owner-operator from Suffolk. When he first started sub-contracting for Kepstowe he got asked to do their regular run to the airport at Moscow for Aeromar. For the next year he stuck doing solely this work and undertook twenty-six trips in the year. Considering the distance and the queues at the borders you could encounter, this was some feat of driving! He would always run Renault trucks, not a manufacturer that others would choose usually on this type of work.

Alan Johnson gave him the nickname Lenin. 'We were coming through the Ruse border between Bulgaria and Romania back when Bulgaria was still communist. A customs officer looked at Alan, pointed to a picture of Vladimir Lenin, then to Alan, and exclaimed "Lenin" with a big grin on his face. I must have mentioned it in passing to one or two of the others, and for some reason it stuck!' He laughs.

One gap in the Russian black market Alan found was for worn-out car tyres. He soon realised that Russian cars were running about on totally bald tyres, with the wires and cords hanging out. Whenever he got home, he would pop to his local tyre and exhaust centre and take away several tyres that were deemed scrap by UK standards but were like new to a Russian worker. Upon arrival in Moscow, these would be swapped on the black market for diesel. This was far quicker and easier than trying to sell them, especially as the local currency at the time was next to useless to everyone, even the locals.

Alan passed away in 2018.

Alan Bremner, aka Lenin, repairing his Renault. (Steve Clark)

David Jamieson

David 'Jamie' Jamieson was a soft-spoken Scotsman who knew Alan Johnson and Steve Clark from their time working together at M&C Transport in Essex. He was an experienced former Middle East driver who had been working for well-known Scottish company Frank White, mostly running to Iran. He had become an owner-driver and bought Alan Johnson's Daf 3300 to set himself up.

Steve recalls one trip with Jamie. 'It was 1992, we had loaded some flat-pack furniture out of somewhere in the sticks close to Moscow and we were heading for home. After leaving the final police checkpoint in what is now Belarus, I heard a really strange noise coming from my truck. After stopping and investigating,

Jamie Jamieson towing Steve Clark's stricken Volvo. He had bought this Daf from Alan Johnson. (Steve Clark)

it was determined to be coming from the gearbox. The decision was made not to carry on driving to prevent possibly causing some irreparable damage. The only slight issue was that Jamie only had a wire strop in his toolbox to help with the 'recovery'. Despite the lack of an actual bar, he managed to tow my stricken Volvo to the Sovtransavto depot at Minsk.

'Once there, we had a chat with the mechanics in their workshop. To get me further along a lot safer we wanted to move the bumper on Jamie's trailer upwards so we could attach a proper straight bar to get me into Poland. The lads in the workshop were fantastic. Not only did they get the bolts off the bumper that we couldn't move, but they also created an A frame bar for us to use. With this on, the truck was secure and stable, and we towed it to the Riders Motel in Poland. Here, I used Wladek's veteran recovery truck to hoist the gearbox out and strip it down for assessment. It turned out the overdrive gear had split, and to get a new one in Poland was going to be expensive with import duties among other issues. As I had a spare gearbox at home, I simply put it back together without the overdrive and got myself home, where I could fix it myself at much less of a cost. If Jamie hadn't been there, then I would have been in for a hell of a long wait, or a pricy recovery job.'

Mick Twemelow

Mick was an owner-operator who has already charted his time with Kepstowe in his own book *The Vodka Cola Cowboy*. Mick was another driver who came from the Pro-Motor stable.

Mick passed away on 8 May 2018.

Ted Harris

Ted was another owner-driver from Essex. He was not a full-time sub-contractor but would step in when required over several years. Initially running a Scania that was not equipped with a night heater, he purchased Alan Douglas's Volvo F16 when Alan bought a newer truck. Despite the working conditions generally being dirty, especially in the winter, Ted would be known to wear white jeans and yet not get himself covered in muck. To get around the filthy job of dismantling the trailer, Ted would stock up before leaving home with small jars of Nescafé coffee. He found that when workers at delivery points were incentivised with a jar of this 'luxury' item, they were more than happy to do the manual labour part on his behalf! Ted passed away in January 2023.

Steve Tovey and Ted Harris parked at the Riders Motel. Ted's 112 didn't have a night heater fitted, which must have made winter work out east extremely difficult! (Steve Tovey)

A ROUGH GUIDE TO OVERLAND DISTANCES

Distance depends on the route through Europe taken at the time, so can only be a rough guide. Also, it needs pointing out that newer roads and routes have been developed in the intervening years. This list is purely so the reader can gauge roughly the distance the trucks travelled.

London–Moscow = 1,800 miles

Moscow–Omsk = 1,680 miles

Moscow–Novosibirsk = 2,100 miles

Moscow–Irkutsk = 3,250 miles

Moscow–Tashkent (capital of Uzbekistan) = 2,100 miles

Moscow–Almaty (Kazakhstan) = 2,500 miles

Moscow–Bishkek (Kyrgyzstan) = 2,300 miles

COUNTRY BY COUNTRY

As with any work in haulage, you always have a choice of route to your destination. With Kepstowe, generally there were two as far as the border with Russia. It would also depend on which day of the week you were departing. Friday sailings from Harwich into Turku in Finland were a luxurious option, and certainly the preferred option by a lot of the drivers. The M/V *Garden* was a freighter that plied this route. This was three days of comparative luxury on board compared with driving. The trucks would have no wear and tear, the drivers would be refreshed and certainly relaxed. As this would become a regular sailing for most, the drivers would be on first-name terms with the staff of the ship. Some were even given guided tours of the bridge, which was quite an eye-opener. Upon disembarkation at Turku on Monday, the border town of Vaalimaa was approximately a four-hour drive. Once there, customs formalities and the exiting out of Finland would take a matter of minutes. Then the Russian border itself was quite quick in comparison with other frontiers across Europe, meaning you could be on your way very much quicker than if you were heading overland through Poland, for example. Using this route meant that Kepstowe could offer an accurate delivery date to its customers.

The cheaper option, however, was always overland. This would start upon arrival at Calais or Zeebrugge, depending on your ferry out of the UK. You would then be transiting through Belgium, Holland, Germany and Poland and onto the border at Brest. This would

Waiting to board the M/V *Garden* at Harwich for the leisurely cruise to Finland. (Steve Clark)

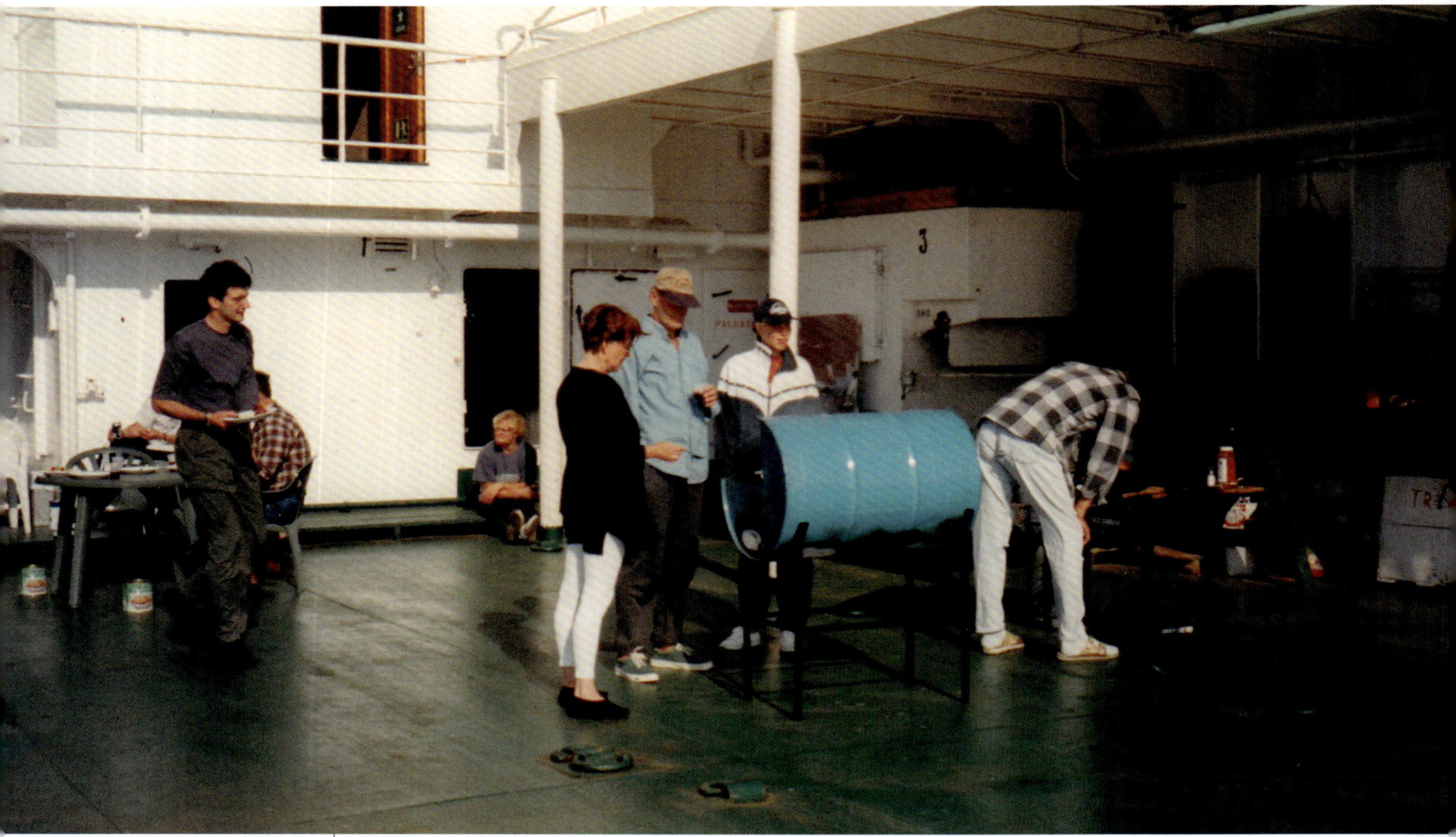

On board the M/V *Garden*, which sailed between Harwich and Turku, Finland. This provided drivers a nice time for some rest and relaxation before hitting the gruelling roads heading east. (Alan King)

also depend on whether you would get through Germany before Sunday. Truck movements are banned there from 10pm on Saturday night until 10pm on Sunday. For the earlier travellers, Germany itself was split into east and west before the fall of the Berlin Wall, which meant even more hostile customs officers, possibly the most suspicious ones that you would encounter. With the frequency of queues, it was harder to gauge the date of arrival of the truck at its destination, so it would be used more for non-urgent loads, or of a less-sensitive nature.

One regular haunt for western drivers either heading outwards or returning home was a truck stop called the Riders Motel located at Siedlce, Poland. Being around 50km to the frontier with Russia, this would be your last port of call heading east, or if returning from Russia, your first chance for a decent shower and meal after battling the border. As with most truck stops at this time, the parking itself was not brick weave cleanliness but a large dirt area, so in the summer it was somewhat dusty, and the winter months would bring plenty of mud. However, it was generally flat and secure. There was a good restaurant, it also boasted a motel, launderette, a workshop and garage. The proprietors also owned a recovery truck to complement the workshop, something they continue to this day. A regular stream of battered and bruised trucks kept them ever busy, and several of the Kepstowe regulars were helped there in their hour of need.

A note should be made here about the conditions of the roads once the drivers had crossed the international border, either into Poland at Frankfurt Oder, or into Russia via Finland. In a word they were horrendous! With the complete lack of investment under the communist regime, the road transport infrastructure was a mess, and that is being generous. Single-track roads were generally the order of

Steve Clark and Chris Everitt with his Iveco join a Kepstowe driver at the Riders Motel. (Steve Clark)

Steve Clark's Daf in need of a wash. (Steve Clark)

the day, and with tarmac breaking and often not being repaired it would lead to a rough ride, and these were the better parts! Theoretically you could let go of the steering wheel and the ruts in the asphalt would take your truck in the right direction, such was their depth. As the drivers got east of Moscow the general driving conditions deteriorated even quicker along with the tarmac.

The M1, but not as we know it. This one runs from Smolensk to Moscow. (Alan King)

Life in the slow lane. Lou gets passed by some local transport while having a break. (Lou Johnson)

The motorway between Minsk and Moscow. The word motorway is a little optimistic … (Steve Clark)

Steve Tovey on the way home from Orel, November 1995. (Steve Tovey)

Another day, another queue. Lou is sat behind a Volvo from the Czech company CSAD, another well-known haulier across Europe. (Lou Johnson)

These roads would cover the trucks in thick layers of glutenous mud and dust, often covering the name on them almost completely. Several of the drivers were turned away from truck washes in Western Europe when heading for home because the trucks were deemed 'too dirty', the owners fearing they would clog up and potentially damage the truck washes. Alan Johnson recalls one trip. 'I was returning one October. It had been snowing in Russia but then melting, which meant a lot of mucky slush which coated the truck and trailer. You could just about see the side windows and where the wipers had been doing their best to keep my forward vision. I got stopped by the Police on the M4 because the truck was so dirty they were curious to where I had been. That particular year had been a bit of an Indian summer and it was still quite warm in the UK, so they were shocked at such a filthy truck on the road. Russia at the time was also somewhere hardly anybody visited so they were quite interested to hear about it.'

In all, Kepstowe provided a comprehensive service throughout the CIS (Commonwealth of Independent States). The only one that was never visited by Kepstowe was Tajikistan, although should a load have been required there, this would have readily been undertaken.

Border Queues

One thing that always comes up when trucking out east and outside of Europe as we know it are the queues at the borders. In the early pioneering days as previously mentioned, Poland was in a state of martial law, which pretty much ended any possibility of transiting. When this ended in 1983, the overland route was taken once again by driver-accompanied trucks. The queues were practically non-existent. With the tight grip on the economy held by the communist regime, there really

Mickey Packham, queueing as usual, for the Russian frontier. (Mickey Packham)

Queueing at the frontier, Brest. (Steve Clark)

The queue at Bobrowniki from Poland into what is now Belarus. Behind Steve in the photo you can see three trucks from Dutch haulier Dakutrans and also just visible is another regular Dutch company heading east, Moeijes. (Steve Tovey)

was not too much trade crossing, and being in a western truck meant you held a trump card. The few trucks waiting were not concerned by your arrival, or even heading in front of them to start your clearance. But as the vice-like grip eased and international trade increased, so did the length of the queues. It morphed into a snake of trucks, often taking several days to get to the front to begin the process of customs clearance. Woe betide you if you fell asleep; when you awoke there was a good chance you would find a different truck in front of you from when you closed your eyes. Your days would consist of a dirty, wide road, with no sign of a shop or garage until you were very close to the border itself. Having your own food and drink supplies was imperative. Local entrepreneurs often saw a captive audience, and would try and flog their wares, from food and drink, often of a dubious quality, to cigarettes or hand-crafted items. Many a driver purchased a small wooden stool to sit on and while away the hours, often just to get themselves left alone by the hopeful seller only for another to come along. If you were after any sort of welfare facilities, this was not the place for you. The thought of a Portaloo was merely that and should such a luxury be added to the roadside, you can imagine what sort of condition that would be in within a matter of days. I personally have encountered such luxuries on my own travels in much more modern times, and let's just say it is best to prepare ahead as best you can!

During the hot summer months, the acrid stench of urine from the tarmac, and worse from the trees and bushes close by, left you wishing it were the winter months again, where snow covers the roads and disguises the assault on the senses. When you finally jostled your way into the customs compound at the head of

Belarussian–Russian border, marked only by a police post at the time, so no need to stop unless instructed. (Steve Clark)

this large snake, you were only halfway there with your battle. The apathy of border guards could be staggering. You must not dare awaken them from their slumber across their desk; they were at work to sleep, not to work. The guards would send you to the next 'control' to obtain the next stamp on your paperwork. If it was your first time navigating this minefield of windows and numbers it could be daunting, especially when you factored in a whole new alphabet to get your head around as well. When you had received all the necessary stamps, had your load inspected and had been asked for the usual 'gift', you were permitted to drive out of the barrier, breathing a sigh of relief. Usually, most important of all, you could now get a decent sleep without fear of losing your place. All this would leave you thinking, 'Why do I do this?' The crossing at Brest from Poland into what is now Belarus became the most notorious for queues. Steve Clark's longest time here was fifty-four hours, Dave Kane queued with Chris Everitt for 22km just as two examples.

The biggest queue Alan Johnson ever managed to jump was around 16km, and this wasn't even at a Russian frontier. Alan recalls, 'Myself and Pete Newlyn were heading back to the UK from Moscow. After loading two consignments of shoes as a back load, we had parked in Poland on the Friday night. Before I turned in for the night, I said I was going to get up early and try and get through the border before the weekend ban. We had got as far as the border at Frankfurt Oder, which is between Poland and Germany, and joined the back of the queue. While we sat there, a German aid convoy started to come past us but fairly well spread out, so I decided to take a chance. I called Pete on the CB, and he was a bit apprehensive, but I just said, "What's the worst that can happen, we get sent back? Come on, nothing ventured nothing gained!" Anyway, we slipped out behind one of the trucks into one of these large gaps and drove right to the front of the queue! When we got to the front, rather than just follow the empty aid trucks, we nipped across into the loaded truck bay area to process the paperwork, which surprised the officials a little bit! We just shrugged our shoulders and pleaded ignorance! Luckily, they didn't really pay us any attention as to how we were suddenly there, and so they stamped our paperwork without too much fuss. Now we were clear from Poland, just Germany to go. A short drive through no man's land so to speak took us into the German side, and they were just as surprised! But, once again they stamped us in without any interest, and we got our feet down hard on the pedals west towards the Netherlands.

What Pete did not know at the time was I had previously found a man in Braintree to make me a signboard for the front of my truck. It was white with a red cross on with 'Help for Russia' written around the cross. Well, it was non-committal and a bit vague, and if need be I would attach this to the front of the truck to help my passage to the front of the queue!'

Russia

The bread-and-butter work for Kepstowe was always to Russia itself. Spanning eleven time zones, it is the world's largest country by quite some margin. Before the collapse of communism, visits were limited to Moscow and Leningrad, now called St Petersburg. There was a ring of security and mistrust meaning no other destinations were available; a lot of the towns were closed off even to their own citizens. Slowly but surely, with capitalism taking its place, the country began to want

Friends on the road. Cyril Gardiner was the driver of the Croome's Volvo. Croome International Transport still exists today. In the background is the iconic Hungarocamion transport company. (Alan Johnson)

more and more from the west, and the trucks would venture further and further into this formerly closed-off country. In the early days, back loads were non-existent. However, as it slowly opened up a few regular jobs would be tried and tested, and become quite a regular commodity. If time allowed, local transport would either collect the consignments or reload empty trailers that had been dropped. If not, the drivers would go and collect themselves. Equipment like ship's mooring lines from Kolomna, south-east of Moscow, would go back to Hamburg. Pianos from Penza, vodka from Kursk, empty beer barrels from the British pub in Moscow, to name a few, meant that trucks would not often be heading west empty.

One of Kepstowe's largest customers was Aeromar. They were the company who provided all the food and logistics to the Russian national air carrier, Aeroflot. Initially Kepstowe were delivering just their foodstuffs from the UK for their international flights. This work quickly became a weekly service from London. The trucks would load fridge trailers from a variety of suppliers, mainly around south London, and then with a final collection from Croydon the trailer would be sealed, a trip back to the Kepstowe HQ for all the paperwork, and then head off east. One thing the drivers liked about this work was not only was there a shower on site in Moscow to use, but also a telephone, a real rarity in Russia at the time. This meant they could let loved ones at home know they had arrived safely to quell any concerns. It also meant they could speak to the London office when they arrived at work to receive their instructions once the trailer was empty.

Alan Bremner ended up spending most of his time on this work, it just seemed to suit him. As he was practically living out of his truck at the time, he would often get

Lou clearing customs at the national carrier Sovtransavto's depot. This took three days to complete. (Lou Johnson)

Nick Reynolds had a lucky escape on sheet ice after being overtaken by a car while trying to manoeuvre around a parked van. (Ian Mellor)

Parked by the Mezhdunarodnaya hotel in Moscow. Pete Newlyn can be seen sat in his F10, and another British truck, owned by Trevor Starkes from Essex, is parked alongside. Behind these a Dutch-registered Daf is visible. Also note the Mercedes car in the foreground was originally German but clearly exported, hence the D sticker on the boot. The hotel is still trading, although any sort of truck parking outside has long since stopped. (Steve Clark)

back into the UK, reload and head back out, or even meet another driver in the west, perform a trailer change and head straight back for the border. One year, as mentioned previously, he undertook twenty-six trips, one a fortnight.

As time went on, Aeromar asked Kepstowe to help supply other items that were required that were more problematic for a Russian company to buy from outside their borders. A fine example of this were two Renault trucks. They were high-lift loaders used at airports, so something that was quite an exclusive build compared to an average tractor unit. These were sourced in

Steve Clark at Sheremetyevo airport, the home of Aeromar in Moscow. (Steve Clark)

Two Renault hi-lift loaders trucks were bought by long-standing customer Aeromar through Kepstowe's, and delivered to Moscow's Sheremetyevo airport. With no sleeper cabs the drivers were put up in hotels. (Steve Clark)

Parked at the Motel Tver. Flanking Alan King, Lou and Nigel Harness is a local Maz truck, and a Bulgarian-registered Mercedes from Somat, the former national carrier that was bought by the giant German company Willi Betz when it was privatised. (Lou Johnson)

France and driven out to be put into service. Matt Towse and the Braintree-based fitter, Paul 'Rab' Jose, had the dubious honour of driving them east. With a lack of sleeper cabs, the duo were 'treated' to hotels every night. 'The word hotel was somewhat optimistic. Grotty shacks would probably describe some of the places a bit better, but I guess it was better than being across the seats with no curtains or night heater,' Matt recalled. 'But at least we only had to go one way with them, and once there it was a flight back and we were home.'

Minsk Mound of Glory war memorial, 21km outside of Minsk on the road to Moscow. (Steve Clark)

A regular hazard of the winter. The Danish driver's fuel filters had frozen, so Steve Clark stopped to lend a hand. (Steve Clark)

Friends on the road. Steve and Alan stop for a break with a Dutchman from Nesotra, Ko van Kooten. (Steve Clark)

To kick off the new year of 1991, Matt and his brother Pat were assigned to an exhibition tour for the worldwide brand Rank Xerox. This would not be taking in any cities in the western part of Europe, however. Most of the equipment had been delivered to the Kepstowe depot in Wandsworth and loaded onto Pat's Volvo F10 Globetrotter. This was coupled to a box trailer that had been liveried with the Rank Xerox name especially for this job. Matt was to drive the Volvo FL4 and accompany his brother. First off was a short hop across the water to Venlo in the Netherlands. It is a town right by the German border. Here, some copier machines were to be loaded and then the duo were good to go. Directly east was the direction of travel, as the first city on the itinerary was Warsaw. From here it was south to Katowice in Poland before heading south again to Prague in the Czech Republic. Onto Bratislava then Budapest before entering Romania, heading for the capital Bucharest. Then it was onto the Black Sea and the port and resort town of Varna in Bulgaria. February by the sea in Europe, however, is not parasols and swim shorts. Then it was on to the capital Sofia from the coast, then into Belgrade and Zagreb. At this time both cities were still part of Yugoslavia. This was the end of the so called 'easy part in Europe'. The next city was Kiev, Ukraine. The route should have been to transit around Budapest in Hungary to the border town of Zahony. However, en route Matt's Volvo FL4 had a clutch failure.

Matt recalled: 'It was snowing like anything of course; you never have

A flat-pack furniture factory for a reload. They had to lift the pipes up with a crane to let his truck in and out. (Steve Clark)

pleasant weather when you break down! We got the truck to Hungarocamion's yard (Hungarocamion were the state-owned transport company of Hungary at the time). It was a Sunday night when we got there, but with time pressing we had to get on. With both trucks equipped with tail lifts and with a couple of pallet trucks, we transhipped everything from my truck onto Pat's. The FL4 was parked up for Kepstowe to sort out when they got in to work on the Monday morning. I jumped into Pat's truck, and we double manned off to the border. When we arrived, there was some confusion. The border guards had never actually seen a British-registered truck before, and thought we were Bulgarian but with the nationality sticker the wrong way around, with our GB and not BG stickers! Once this confusion was sorted out it was the usual border affair, getting all the right stamps in all the right places. Soon enough we were on our way.'

After Kiev, only two cities were left to visit, Moscow and Leningrad. With the end of this run, it was a case of getting back to the UK to unload all the equipment and wait and see what job was on the cards next. All in, this had taken just about two months to complete. The FL4 in the meantime had been repaired and brought back to the UK by another Kepstowe driver.

Loading the furniture by hand all day. Somewhere between Moscow and Latvia. (Steve Clark)

Right and below: Delivering equipment for the building of a new petrol station with Chris Everitt. Stripping the trailers out like this for a crane to unload can be laborious and difficult, especially in the bitter winter when the canvas of the tilt becomes like a sheet of cardboard. Steve remembers this delivery being bitterly cold, but having a colleague to help with this trailer dismantling method makes it a sight easier. (Steve Clark)

PepsiCo in Russia

The global, American-owned brand Pepsi had managed to open a plant in the then Soviet Russia in 1974 in Novorossiysk, and by the end of 1982, there were a further seven more plants across the USSR.

After 1991, when Russia had opened up, Pepsi planned on expanding its facilities further, building four more plants located in Novosibirsk, Krasnoyarsk, Samara and Ekaterinburg with more cities earmarked for possible development. All these plants would be requiring trucks to be based there for distribution, and this is where Kepstowe stepped in.

The trucks all came from the Republic of Ireland. This was down to one man, Richard Sheridan. Richard had been working for the rival company Coca-Cola in Dublin and had subsequently been headhunted by Pepsi. Once settled into his new job, he was tasked with improving the Russian side of the business.

He had previously dealt with Tommy Keenan of Keenan Trailers, and asked if he could supply him with the equipment required.

'When people heard I was selling trailers to Russia, most of them laughed and said that I would never get paid, and pretty much what a fool I was. What they didn't know, however, was that every trailer was bought and paid for before it even got on a ferry across to England,' Tommy recalls with a wry smile.

For the tractor units, Tommy spoke to his long-term friend Oliver McElvaney at McElvaney Scania, based at Finglas, Dublin. He was happy to find the trucks, or even supply new when second-hand options were thin on the ground.

'All the trailers were 40ft Gray and Adams refrigerated units. At the time, everybody was switching to the new approved 45ft trailers, so there was a broad choice for Richard to choose from. Some were left in their previous colours, mostly plain white, but others we were asked to paint blue and add the livery to.'

Alan Johnson, between by Steve Holding in the Pepsi-liveried Scania, and Michael Mudie. (Alan Johnson)

Pepsi's plant in Samara. The Lada has yellow licence plates but a Russian registration, denoting that the owner is a non-national. (Mickey Packham)

Finnish drivers with Richard Warren in Samara delivering on behalf of Pepsi. They couldn't find the factory because it wasn't built yet! Richard double chained his truck and shunted everyone's trailers into position for delivery rather than everyone chain their own trucks. (Steve Clark)

One of the prepared Scanias outside McElvaney Scania awaiting collection. (Adrian McElvaney)

Ian Mellor on his first trip to Russia. (Dave Button)

Dave Button with the Irish-sourced Scania. (Dave Button)

The trucks themselves came down from McElvaney's truck centre at Monaghan. All were left-hand drive but were in a variety of power outputs and cab specifications, because of the requirements and what was available for sale at the time. Any 3 series Scania would be second-hand; however, the newer 4 series trucks were all brand new and specified for their harsh future in the east. In total close to forty trucks and trailers left the shores of Ireland for the east. Tasked with delivering the trucks to the plants, some drivers had to be found. At the time, all their regular drivers had their own dedicated trucks, and as these would be left in situ and the drivers flown home, a couple of fresh faces were required. Some of the combinations were driven to Harwich and sent without a driver, and some Finnish drivers took them onwards. But two British drivers were also found. These were Ian Mellor and Steve Harding.

Ian had previously worked with Dave Button on the Middle East run, and when Dave was asked by the office if he knew of anyone looking for some work, he gave Ian a call, and got him on board.

The first two trucks that were sent were plain white 3 series Scanias, which Dave and Ian were tasked with delivering. Although Dave had his own truck at the time, he was asked to run with Ian to show him the ropes on his first run. The delivery address was Novosibirsk, geographical centre of Russia.

The trucks were collected from the Braintree satellite yard. They had been shipped over previously and delivered by two Irishmen who had since flown home. There was never an actual load inside the trailers, but often spare parts for the vehicles or sometimes some advertising paraphernalia were on board. This meant that realistically there should be two carnets with the vehicle, one for the truck and one for the load. However, this never caused an issue at any of the borders.

On this first trip, there was a problem with the air drier on Ian's truck. This was cured when they jammed some cardboard between the radiator and the intercooler. Aside from this problem, their inaugural run went smoothly without other issues.

Not all the Pepsi trucks were second-hand, some were brand new. Ian took this photo deep inside Russia. (Ian Mellor)

Ian parked next to Chris Everitt's Iveco. (Ian Mellor)

The only tank container required was this one. Note the branding was in Cyrillic on this truck. This was delivered to the plant at Samara. (Ian Mellor)

Alan Johnson a long way from anywhere, heading for Irkutsk. (Alan Johnson)

Journey's end. Dave arrives at the town of Irkutsk, a little over 5,000km from Moscow and 8,000km from London. (Dave Button)

On arrival in Novosibirsk, Dave and Ian stopped when they saw a policeman to ask some directions. 'Good afternoon gentlemen,' the policeman greeted them in clipped English. 'Bloody hell, you can speak English,' Ian spluttered. If he had a mouthful of tea it would have been on the ground at this point. 'Indeed, my father was Scottish and a sailor by trade. How may I help you, are you lost?' The friendly boy in blue, quite a rare find anywhere in Russia, soon gave them the directions they required and off the duo set to the factory gates of Coca Cola! 'Not sure we are exactly at the right place,' remarked Dave.

The Pepsi factory that was being built in Irkutsk would prove to be the furthest point that the drivers would get to overland. Dave Button recalls his journey vividly.

'On 4 July 1997, I shipped out from Harwich to Turku as usual. It was a

Dave Button en route to Irkutsk. (Dave Button)

relatively simple run, with two drops in Moscow and then onto Nizhny Novgorod, which is about 400km to the east of the capital. I then returned to Moscow to reload, and once that was complete it was back to Turku, arriving there around 19 July. While waiting for the ferry, I received a message asking if I would go straight back east rather than to the UK. I was informed the destination was Irkutsk, Siberia. Being as I love doing the longer trips, I agreed readily. The trailer arrived on the 22nd, and I set off for the border and the start of my longest trip across Russia, a little over 6,000km from the docks. This took me eleven days of heading east, with nine days of that heading east from Moscow alone. The routine was drive, sleep, drive, sleep every day. Being out of the scope of European tachograph laws gave me a bit more leeway to get some distance covered once I was out of Finland, but the roads were a mixture of tarmac, dust and gravel track. Once east of the Ural Mountains, often gravel track was the course of the day. All in all, despite doing slightly longer days, I did not really gain much at all. When I got there, I was eight hours ahead of Greenwich mean time! Thankfully it was not the middle of winter, so the driving conditions were a little more favourable.

'I remember approaching the police post at Irkutsk, and one of the policemen rushing out with his lollipop to stop me. 'Here we go again,' I thought, more money to pay for some fictitious reason. But as it turned out, he had received instructions to stop me and call Pepsi so they could send a car to guide me in. I hadn't seen any European spec trucks for several days, so this policeman wouldn't have had any trouble recognising me coming down the road. He was very nice, he even made me a cup of tea, but he didn't believe I was English. He simply could not get his head around the fact that I had driven there from so far away. It was a Friday afternoon when I arrived, and they were not planning on unloading me until the Monday, so I spent the weekend in Irkutsk. Some of the British engineers from Pepsi invited me to Lake Baikal with them. Here was an opportunity not to miss, get away from the truck for the day, and visit the world's deepest and oldest lake. It certainly helped to make the weekend pass quickly.

'On the Monday after unloading, I started heading back west towards Moscow. I had a power steering problem on the way back though, exactly where I cannot remember. One of the hose joints had come loose and the truck lost a lot of power steering fluid.

Utilising the drivers' tractor units to provide anchoring for the stage to stop it blowing over! You can just make out the lines attached to the front. (Steve Clark)

It is one of those issues where you don't know anything is wrong until the steering suddenly gets very heavy. Fortunately, I'd not long before gone through a fairly large village that had a typical Russian local market on the roadside. I remembered seeing some car parts at one of the shops, so I pulled over to the side of the road. Out with the spanners, fix the loose joint (it was a case of simply tightening it up again thankfully). I then dropped the trailer and headed back to the town in the tractor unit. I managed to buy several tins of power steering fluid and regain my steering thankfully. The condition of the roads really meant you didn't want to be without it for long.

'I travelled empty back to Moscow, to the Kepstowe depot, where I dropped my empty trailer, picked up a loaded one, and headed west again. This time I travelled back overland via what is now Belarus into Europe. I finally arrived back at Kepstowe HQ in London on 22 August. What a round trip that was!'

Six drivers took part in a promotional event for Pepsi. These were Mickey Packham, John Mantle, Steve Clark, Chris Everitt, Pete Newlyn and Dave Button. It was put on in two cities where they had recently finished building new plants, partly as a thank you to the workers and their new workforce, and also for some good old-fashioned PR. This celebration seemed to be at a strange time, however; they were to take place near to the beginning of winter, and it was freezing cold! The first show was in Novosibirsk, followed by one in Nizhny Novgorod. The show featured an English Blues Brothers tribute band, followed by some Russian entertainers with some games with prizes, followed by the finale of the Blues Brothers film itself.

'We took everything that they would need, the staging, all the lighting equipment, a big video screen, etc. The assembly crew would arrive either by rail or by plane and get to work. Us drivers would also chip in and give them a hand

The stage almost set out in Novosibirsk. Note the people's attire, not exactly outdoor show weather. (Steve Clark)

with the more basic tasks. It gave us something to do rather than sit about in the cab for even longer.'

The atmosphere got very strange in Nizhny Novgorod, however. They had to drive a couple of the trucks onto the pitch to anchor the video screen down. As the wind had picked up, the screen was acting like a sail and almost threatened to take off! 'We had set it all up at one end of the pitch. The reason for this was that all the public could then use the rest of the pitch for all the dancing and games and so on. However, the army would not let them onto the pitch at all. They all had to sit in the seats around the edge, which ruined it for everyone really. To

Alan King having an al fresco wash at a Russian truck stop. He remembers this day clearly as it was the day his first grandson was born. He received the news via Chris Everitt's in-cab phone. (Alan King)

The three amigos! Mick Ashby can be seen in front of his Volvo, and Chris Everitt in the seat of his Iveco. (Alan King)

see all these performers putting their heart and soul into their act while their audience were nowhere near, and not allowed to enjoy themselves, really put a damper on the whole shindig,' Steve remembers.

Alan King, Mike Ashby and Dave Kane took out a water filtration machine and associated ancillaries to the Pepsi plant in Ekaterinburg. Leaving on Friday, 28 March 1997, the trip would end up taking about a month.

'We shipped out on the M/V *Garden*, arriving in Finland on April Fool's Day, but despite this everything was going fairly smoothly,' Mike recalls, looking back through his old work diaries.

'It took us eight days from Turku to the plant. Once we got there, it took three days for the loads to clear customs so we could unload. Dave was the first to offload as he had a container and headed off back to Moscow for his reload. Alan and I had tilt trailers which we had to dismantle to unload and rebuild. Eventually, with that sorted, all we had to do was "go around the corner", so to speak, as we had a reload from Ekaterinburg. For this part, Chris Everitt was to join us. Chris had previously undertaken a trip to Moscow, reloaded and taken this trailer to Turku for shipment back to the UK. He had collected an empty low-loader trailer that had been shipped for him and headed to join the others in Ekaterinburg. This though took another two days for the paperwork to be ready and for it to also be cleared by customs, talk about frustrating! The man in charge of the loads kept coming out to us and complaining about us being sat about. We explained again and again that we would much rather be getting some kilometres under our belts instead of sitting about waiting, but that is the procedure, and there was not much that we could do but wait!

'Eventually, we got the green light to get going. Chris, having the low-loader, was loaded with a large machine, and Alan and I had all the assorted ancillaries to make it work. This meant going back over the hills of the Urals was slow going with the weight Chris was dragging. Our final destination was Zurich, so we were heading out via Finland. I remember getting back to Tver on 10 April, and it was still snowing, I was wondering if winter would ever bloody end! Once we got back into Finland,

Tver, April and yet there is still snow around. Chris, Alan and Mike parked alongside a local's Kamaz truck. (Mike Ashby)

we took the thirty-hour ferry from Helsinki to Rostock and disembarked. With Chris's load needing permits this meant we got weekended as we could not get anything arranged until the Monday. Finally, Monday came around and we got motoring down to Switzerland, got cleared of customs and got unloaded. I had a feeling if we waited too long, they would find reloads for us from Italy, and that would mean more delays. I could stomach them in Russia where they were the norm and you were a long way from home, but I didn't want to lose time in Italy with this trip so I set off north and called the office once inside of Germany. "Oh right, well you may as well come back if you are already there," was the response, that was music to my ears, and we hot-footed it empty back to Calais to get ourselves home.'

Richard Warren

After buying a second-hand truck from his friend Nigel Fry, owner of a company called Traction GB (another Kent-based haulier), Richard put this to work heading east. H2 TGB was a Scania 113, converted with an aftermarket high roof by Dutch company Estepe. The high-roof conversion gave a lot more living space, something most trucks at the time were desperately lacking. On his first trip in his new truck however, all didn't quite go to plan.

'Belarus had just become independent from Russia, and they had put up a border to the south of Smolensk at a town called Orsha. The queue for this was huge, which was no real change for Russia though, so I lost several days just waiting in among this. Sadly, I also lost my clutch as well! I managed to get a message through to the Kepstowe office in Moscow, and they told me they would send some people to help me. This was in the winter of course; these things never happen in the summer do they? It was cold, very cold, and everything froze; the diesel, batteries, my tins of food, and me myself! I slept in every item of clothing I had with me, along with my coat and in two sleeping bags and waited for help to arrive. In the meantime, contact was also made with Nigel, who I had just bought the truck from. Without hesitation, he bought a new clutch and all the ancillaries required to get it fixed. Considering he could have had the attitude of 'sorry, sold as seen', he didn't want us thinking that he would sell a truck

Richard Warren kicking up the dust en route to Novosibirsk. (Richard Warren)

that was not in tip-top condition, and full credit to him for going above and beyond in our hour of need. After what seemed like a lifetime, Steve Makin and Geoff Burton (Geoff was working for another sub-contractor) arrived, put me in one of their cabs to warm up first, and when we couldn't get it repaired, Steve towed my truck and trailer on a bar to the Riders Motel. There Wladek, the owner, took the truck to his personal farm to fix it.

'Nick Reynolds, meanwhile, had collected all the parts required from Nigel back in the UK and was heading for Moscow, so he dropped them all off when he passed. Apart from being so cold – I honestly think it is the coldest I have ever been in my life – one other thing sticks out in my mind like nothing else. When we had all the new parts there ready and waiting, Wladek was putting it all together again for me. All of a sudden, he grabbed a wooden stool and smashed it onto the frozen ground. Now he was not a small man to say the least, and I was guessing he was really frustrated by something. However, he had done this for a reason. He picked up one of the legs of the stool and took it off to his lathe. He proceeded to mill a spigot out of the leg to line the clutch up when fitting it. Polish ingenuity at its best!'

Dave Button and Alan King took two trailers on separate occasions to a private dacha situated on the outskirts of Moscow. A dacha is a privately owned summer house for the more affluent Russians. It was in the middle of a pine forest, not ideal for finding on your road map. The house was being refurbished and the owners had bought as many British-made items as they could. The duo delivered everything required, including the kitchen sink!

Dave recalls: 'I cannot remember where exactly the house was located, but I was met somewhere outside Moscow by the usual Lada containing the archetypal

Much cheaper than buying it at a garage, although the quality of the diesel can leave something to be desired. But sometimes needs must and you have to do what you have to just to keep on trucking ... (Steve Tovey)

large Russians in leather coats and fur hats. They led me deep into the forest to the dacha on tracks made for a Kamaz (a Russian-built, off-road truck) rather than a Volvo that I was driving. The rumour was that it was owned by a former KGB officer who now owned a private security company, but I do not know how true that was.

'The load was all sorts of high-end household furnishings, from carpets to furniture and plenty of boxes marked fragile. Every one of these I saw I wondered just how they would have fared with a Russian-built truck rather than the ones we were driving. Looking back at it now, although not all of it originated from Harrods, I believe a lot of it had done. The men unloading and doing all the work on site were British. I recognised some of them from some of the British Council jobs I had been involved with previously.

'I was not allowed on the site at all, I was instructed to stay in my cab until I was told otherwise. When the trailer was empty, I was told that I could go. Problem was, the Lada that had brought me in had long since disappeared, and I had to find my own way out.

'Now I have normally got a good sense of direction. But, as one Russian tree and snow-covered track looks pretty much the same as any other, I was somewhat uncertain of my escape route. 'Just follow your tracks from when you came in,' I can hear you saying. This was easier said than done though. To a certain extent I could, but because I had been there several hours, fresh snow had fallen and other vehicles driving around the area over the tracks I had made getting in meant it wasn't quite that easy. Adding into the mix, I had to reverse back down the lane I was in and around a 90-degree turn, now with no weight in the trailer either. Let's just

Below and opposite: Dave Button delivering to the Dacha in the winter time of 1995. Alan King certainly got the better end of the deal! (Dave Button)

KEPSTOWE
FREIGHT SERVICES LTD.
Tel 081 871 4426
Telex 923597
F12

Right and below: Alan King delivering to the private dacha somewhere in the woods outside of Moscow. Access was somewhat tight, but the weather conditions were a sight better than what Dave Button had to endure on the same delivery site the previous year! (Alan King)

say it was an interesting journey back to a tarmac road, which I was very pleased to see before it got dark!'

Alan fared a lot better with this delivery, however, as his was undertaken roughly six months later. 'There wasn't a flake of snow to be seen. The forest was well and truly alive, and I distinctly remember the overwhelming smell of the pine trees. It was a beautiful site, ideal for having a summer bolt hole. I was a little apprehensive after what I heard Dave had endured, but with the advantage of daylight and the better weather, it was one of my more enjoyable deliveries I have to say, sorry Dave!' Alan reminisces with a chuckle.

The furthest north Richard Warren got to be was a town called Syktyvkar in the Komi Republic. It is approximately 1,300km north-east of Moscow. The cargo this time was incubators and hospital equipment for premature babies, donated by the Wellcome Trust.

'It would have been easier if there was a road,' Richard laughs! 'I had driven until I was pretty close to the destination, but I was struggling to find the exact building. Suddenly, a Lada with a large "L" plate on its roof stopped in front of me, and a man got out of the passenger seat. It turns out he was a driving instructor with a pupil under tuition. Her lesson instantly became giving me directions to the hospital. The reason I struggled to find it is because in true Soviet design chic, the place looked like every other building about, and more like a steel works than a children's hospital. Gas pipes running up the outside, rusty metal bars on some windows and so on. I remember it being a Saturday when I arrived there, but no one was really expecting me. Eventually they managed to find me a doctor who spoke English so I could explain why I was there; everyone was looking flummoxed at the English man who was here with equipment for them. It was decided that unloading would happen the next day, or possibly the Monday, nobody was certain.

'The doctor invited me back to his flat for tea. I tried to decline, but he was so insistent that it seemed rude to say no. I asked if I could get a shower when I was there. His brow furrowed and he said he would see if it were possible. I was thinking to myself that surely this was not too big a question, but when I got to the flat, I soon found out. The word flat is used somewhat loosely. Considering he was a high up doctor, it consisted of a living room that doubled as the bedroom, a tiny kitchen with one electric hob and a sink. There was no sign of a bathroom and certainly not a shower. He then proceeded to make a few phone calls to various people, and then turned to me. It had been arranged that I could use the flats' sinks to wash in in about two hours' time. I had no idea these people shared hot water, sinks, showers and all. I was truly humbled by his kind gesture of getting the whole apartment block's water routine changed so I could have a wash, something I took for granted at home.

'On the Sunday, he came to visit me in the truck to report that nothing would happen until the Monday, and asked if there was anything else he could help with. I asked if it would be possible to use a phone to call home to report everything was OK. He took me to the municipal post office building and began to talk to the lady behind the desk. She then went off, and another man appeared, and he started talking to him. This went on, and on, and on! We had been stood there for about two hours when I was ushered through to the manager's office in the building. In there I was told that I could happily place a call home on Wednesday afternoon at 4pm. Clearly the talks had gone up and up the chain of command to get permission. I had no idea that to make an international call would require booking the line several days in advance, so the call could go to Moscow to be connected to an international line. I was truly humbled by their generosity, but I knew I would hopefully be back beyond Moscow on my way back by then, so I had to decline their offer despite what they had been through just for me. It really did make me appreciate what we took for granted back home and how much tougher all the population had it there at the time.'

John Mantle had a once in a lifetime experience of crossing a frozen river in his truck.

'I had a consignment of gas-analysing equipment for delivery to the town of Nefteyugansk. This was a very new town, which had been founded in 1967 when they discovered oil and gas reserves here, and so the town was really to serve the workers and the industry. To get there I went east from Moscow to Ekaterinburg, where I picked up the trail north. To get to the town from most directions, you have to cross the river Ob. This relatively unknown river is the seventh biggest in the world, so it is no small stretch of water in most places to traverse. My route while loaded would take in a "bridge". I use this term rather loosely as it was a typical Russian affair of barges chained and secured together, along with a toll to cross, of course. They were frozen into the ice, however, so although they were steady enough when you drove on them, traction wise it was a bit of a nightmare as you were driving on bare steel! With this safely crossed, I carried on and found my delivery point. From here I was to head back to the Moscow depot. Being as I was empty, however, meant that I could save at least 100km by driving across the river. I had seen it signposted on my way to the delivery, just a small sign saying Yekaterinburg with a wooden hut and a barrier, so made a mental note of where it was. Upon my return, I pulled up to the hut and paid the babushka lady inside. It was half the price of the barge crossing, so I drove down and onto the ice. The snow was heaped up about halfway either side of the truck. The crossing itself was roughly one mile in length. It was enjoyable taking this rare opportunity of something totally different in a truck. When I reached the bank on the other side, I found to my amazement there was also a toll for crossing the river like this. It was banded as an "ecology tax", talk about a mickey take! My truck at the time was only a year or two old, so was very environmentally friendly, especially when put up against the decrepit local trucks the Russians were using on a daily basis, belching out black smoke and dropping oil. But these were exempt from this tax for some strange reason …!'

Steve Clark, Pete Newlyn and Michael Mudie had three out of gauge loads to take to Kazan in the depths of one winter. 'It was bitterly cold, and snow everywhere, typical Russian winter scene,' Steve recalls. 'We were getting close to Kazan, but due to the bad weather we missed the sign that pointed us across the river Volga towards the city. Oblivious to this we carried on regardless when out of nowhere we found ourselves on some brand-new dual carriageway. After the crap roads we had been enduring, this was surreal. We must have driven at least 50 or 60 miles until it abruptly came to an end, went over a railway crossing and ended at a T-junction. Pete got out and spoke to the lady who was in the level crossing booth, who informed him that we could turn left and go onto the frozen river, or right and head into a railway yard. A tough choice, but we chose the latter and headed into this yard. Driving on a frozen river may be alright in a car, but I very much doubt our trucks would have survived it!

'When the train arrived, we were going to load the trucks onto open carriages to take us to Kazan. First off, the locomotive uncoupled and drew alongside us all, so we could all buy some nice cheap diesel! Then he connected back up ready to take us back to Kazan. The crates that were our loads were a bit higher and wider than your average truck. We tried to warn the driver, but he didn't seem fazed in the slightest. We set off, and after about fifteen minutes or so we came to a stop. This was at a station, where we had to get out of our trucks, walk across a dozen or so railway lines to the ticket office and buy our train tickets! With them in our hands the train carried on. My truck had been the first of the three loaded, and when we came hurtling towards a bridge that we were going under, I literally ducked and waited for the huge bang because it looked so low, yet the train hadn't slowed down in the slightest. Thankfully, somehow, we cleared it, and made our way into Kazan itself.

'The next hurdle was getting us off the railway cars. For some reason this marshalling yard was on a slight curve instead of dead straight, which doesn't make any sense to any other country but then this was Russia. With the slight curve, and the fact that our low-loader trailers had the axles right at the back of the trailer, made it a real pain in the backside to get back onto terra firma. Eventually somehow, we managed it though, and got ourselves into town to unload. It was certainly not your ordinary truck train, and one we never imagined we would find ourselves on either!'

A Long Way Empty

Rod Withers enjoyed this particular job. The British Council was helping with the building of a municipal library in the city of Omsk. It was mostly the prefect's office and his assistants that they were helping with building. The rest was dealt with by the Russian authorities. Being as it was the British Council, all the items were to be imported from the UK, from the plasterboard to the wall paint and so on. The trailer was loaded in Rye, Sussex, from a builder's merchants and Rod set off east.

'First, I had to go to Moscow and unload some of the equipment at the British Council there. The next step was to collect an armed guard for the journey. To be honest I was not too impressed with having to share my cab with anyone, let alone someone I could not easily chew the fat with to pass the time. This was part of the agreement with the job though, so I had to grin and bear it.

'The route to Omsk back then was as good as impassable sticking to just Russia, it was far easier to cut in and out of Kazakhstan, via a town called Petropavl. The only downside to doing this was that the trailer did not have a seal on it anymore due to the offloading in Moscow. Fortunately, with the armed guard to act as a translator for almost any language barrier we came up against, we managed to talk our way through the police checkpoints and borders, with the aid of a few packets of cigarettes, of course! The only real problem truck wise en route was that the air tank's brackets snapped due to vibrations. This was easily remedied by ratchet strapping them to the chassis as a temporary repair until I could find someone with a welder.

'Upon arrival at the building site in Omsk, it was a case of reverse into the site to unload the trailer, drop it on site and go and park the tractor unit up. Then I had to go and pick it up the next day. At the time the trailer was brand new and on its first trip out east. For legal reasons all trailers have various reflectors and stickers down the sides and across the back. When I got back on the site the following morning, all the reflectors had gone missing overnight. Of course no one knew anything about this, but strangely all the local children's push bikes seemed to have smart British-looking reflectors in their wheels!

'Once I had unloaded the trailer, I was told to head back to the Kepstowe depot in Moscow. This time, cutting through the small part of Kazakhstan was a lot easier with the trailer being empty, and we barely lost any time. Once back into Russia, however, the truck's diesel tanks' straps snapped due to the condition of the roads out east. I decided to stop for lunch at a fuel station that also had a garage operating behind it to see if anything could be done with the truck's mechanical issues. When I pulled in, an old, decrepit-looking car pulled in behind me, and three men got out. The security guard and I got chatting with the men as they had come over, and suddenly one of them pulled a gun out, pointed it at me, and told me to get into the cab. The two of us jumped into the truck, and this man demanded some money from me. I told him that I had spent all my money on the diesel in the trailer's belly tank, and I would not have any more money until I arrived back in Moscow. The armed guard I had with me was outside minus his gun, which he had left in his little bag that was still inside the truck. So much for him being there to help me! I showed him my wallet, which had twenty old German Deutschmarks inside, which convinced him I was telling the truth, so he gave up his heist. Little did he know that there was no way I would keep my running money in easy sight out here; it was all tucked away under the bunk and well hidden. With this the men got in their car and set off. I was more annoyed than scared, and I wanted to chase them and run them off the road, but the truck also had an air leak so by the time the air had built up to release the brakes they were long gone. Frustrated by all of this and determined to make the best of a bad situation, I wandered into the garage to see if there was anything they could do repair wise to the tank straps as well as the air tank brackets. I showed him the problem, he said he could fix it, and I negotiated the hefty repair price of a four-pack of Foster's lager!

'After all this excitement, the rest of the trek west to Moscow was somewhat uneventful. Meeting up with several Dutch trucks taking cigarettes back to the Netherlands gave me some travelling companions to share a coffee with as we crossed back across the Ural mountains. Arriving in Moscow, after getting myself cleaned and fed, I was told that there were no loads heading back west at the time, so I may as well head back into Poland and make contact again to see what had come in work wise in the intervening time. Getting back into Europe through the border at Brest once again was not too much of an issue with the trailer still empty, and I was soon pulling back into the Riders Motel parking lot. After a good sleep, a few beers and some food, I contacted the Kepstowe office in London. There was still nothing in the pipeline load wise, so I was asked to head back into Germany and once again call in. I set off west once again and got through the Polish–German border at Frankfurt Oder, headed for Berlin to an Autohof, and once again made contact. (An Autohof is a large rest area for motorists, with a good, large restaurant and parking for all-sized vehicles.) The day was a Thursday, and once again I dialled the numbers to speak to London. The voice on the other end said: "There is a load down at Frankfurt am Main, but it is not loading until Monday, could you go and collect that?" As I had already been out for several weeks, and I could pretty much smell the home cooking across the Channel, I said I would rather just head back empty as I could be home for the weekend. To my surprise, they agreed and so I headed back to Dover empty, all the way from Omsk! In total the trip had taken me three weeks and the next truck to go on the same run took six weeks to complete.'

In 1997, the city of Moscow celebrated its 850th anniversary. The event was commissioned by the mayor, Yuri Luzhkov. This celebration, named 'Saint George, the Bell and the Dragon', was a large pageant held in Red Square, opening on 5 September. Featuring a cast of over a thousand and including horses, there was classical, folk and choral music. Several military bands also took to the stage, as well as actors, poets and a host of other artists. The spectacle would be spread over three days and be broadcast live on television across Russia and the other countries of the CIS. The sale of the broadcast rights were handled by Luzhkov, who owned the Russian channel Central TV that was to broadcast the spectacular. The opera singer Luciano Pavarotti was flown in to sing as one of the main attractions. Originally, he was supposed to be performing in the opening ceremony, however he had to postpone his visit to attend the funeral of Princess Diana and so arrived on Sunday, 7th to participate in the closing ceremonies instead.

Alan King and Dave Kane were contracted to take two generators out to supply the power for the festivities, which involved them being in situ for the whole week. Collecting them from Rockhampton in Gloucestershire, the duo headed to Harwich. Sailing on 22 August, they had the usual leisurely three-day ferry crossing on the M/V *Garden* into Finland. Once into Russia itself, they headed to Sokolniki Park, situated to the north-east of Moscow, to await final customs clearance. This took three days, but the quiet leafy surroundings made the time fly past. 'Much better than most TIR dust bowl parking areas,' Dave remarked with a smile.

On 29 August, the men and their trucks set off for the centre of Moscow under police escort. Upon arrival, they were to be parked and remain attached to the trailers with the generators in the iconic Red Square, right outside St Basil's Cathedral. Another British truck from a rival firm, Fransen Transport, also arrived with them to provide catering supplies for the event. A third British company, sadly no longer trading, Redburn Transfer, bought Pavarotti's equipment out from the UK overland. Alongside these, the British Broadcasting Corporation had a mobile recording studio trailer on site for broadcasting. It had arrived on board an enormous Antonov aeroplane, alongside several other trailers full of equipment that had been sent from England. These behemoths were built in Ukraine during the 1980s, and are some of the heaviest aircraft ever built. Capable of a take-off weight of 640 tonnes, a few trailers of equipment would not test the capabilities of one of these giants of the sky. Neil Pettit from Redburns had collected the mobile studio from the airport on its arrival.

Sokolniki Park, Moscow, awaiting a police escort into Red Square. (Alan King)

The GUM store in Red Square. (Alan King)

Gifts donated by the USA. (Alan King)

Parked right by St Basil's in Red Square. (Alan King)

Part of the show being tested prior to the festivities. (Alan King)

When the extravaganza was over, Dave and Alan were asked if they could assist with transporting some of the trailers to the airport for them to be loaded onto the plane. The Redburn trucks had departed before the actual event so they were the only two trucks available to help. Jumping at the chance, they left their generators on site in Red Square and off they set for the airport. This would provide a rare chance to see one of these planes up close and in operation.

'It was fascinating,' Alan remembers. 'Just to see it up close, dwarfing a truck was impressive, everything about it was massive. Inside, all the chains and loading restraints were made from titanium; it must have cost a fortune when it was originally built. It was little experiences like this that made the job great fun.'

Right and opposite: The impressive sight of the Antonov the trucks were supplying. (Alan King)

Monday the 8th soon came around, and with everything packed away and ready to go, the duo set off for home, westward to Tver, and onwards to Finland. Upon arriving in Finland, they found out they would have the simple route home, mostly at sea. Leaving Helsinki port, they sailed to Stockholm, Sweden, then drove south-west to the city of Gothenburg, where they caught a ferry back into Harwich. Landing back on Sunday, 14 September, it was simply a case of unloading the generators and returning home to Essex.

Loaded in Moscow with the satellite for Italy. (Danny McAuliffe)

Taking a break in France with the pilot vehicle that had escorted him from his arrival back in Harwich. (Danny McAuliffe)

Danny McAuliffe had the unusual job of collecting a satellite from the Russian space programme and trucking it down to Italy. Due to its height, the route was rather straightforward if somewhat unorthodox. From the collection point near Moscow, it was to travel overland to Finland. He caught the boat directly back into the UK, where he then headed into France via Dover, and straight down into Italy. 'It was certainly easier than all the borders I would have encountered and the clattering along the old eastern roads too. The roads through France are like driving on carpet in comparison with them, so I think it would have done the electronics in the satellite a world of favours going the longer way around,' Danny recalls.

Danny with his Italian police escort in the shadow of the Alps. (Danny McAuliffe)

Monsters of Rock, Moscow 1991

September in 1991 found Russia in a state of heightened tension. With a failed coup in August, the people were restless and change was in the air. The powers that be decided to put on a music show that might help ease some of this tension. This led to the Monsters of Rock franchise being asked to organise the show. With it being such a last-minute addition to touring bands' schedules, the logistics of this tested every company involved. However, with good communication, teamwork and knowledgeable people, the show went ahead. It would go down in rock music history, with more than one and a half million people attending.

Alan Johnson took equipment out for this spectacle and Nick Reynolds was also on site with the Fleetwood mobile recording studio. Transam Trucking had empty trucks racing from Barcelona to Moscow from AC/DC's tour. Alan recalls: 'While I had been at home after my last run east, someone had tried to steal my truck from the yard. They failed, but while trying to hotwire it, the starter motor had caught fire and caused a bit of damage. Having to get this repaired meant I missed my next scheduled job for Aeromar, which annoyed me because the airport work could be turned around quickly, meaning you could get home, have your time off and back out again sooner, which meant you could earn better money month by month. I had also missed the coup d'état, which I would like to have witnessed in person, especially as it turned into such a turning point in the country's history.

'As soon as my truck was back up and running, I called the office, and they asked me to take this particular trailer out to Moscow. I loaded it from somewhere around London but cannot recall where; the consignment was a load of video and film equipment. I set off as usual heading out to Poland and for the border. Before I had set off, I had been told by the office that the

Below and opposite: Backstage at the Monsters of Rock music event in Moscow. (Alan Johnson)

Russian president had authorised a letter to be handed out so that all the trucks could get through the border without a problem, and without delay. I knew that anyone at the border who saw this would probably laugh and say it was a fake, so I took it with me, but left it under the bunk, for it to never see the light of day again! Being as we used this border all the time, I knew people's faces and they knew me, so it was not really an issue getting through compared with any other job. The destination was Tushino airfield, which was an old military site. Kepstowe were handling all of the customs clearance for the touring bands' equipment, Fleetwood's mobile studio as well as everything else, so it was all hands on deck for the office staff. When I arrived, the truck was unloaded, and then the trailer was to be used as a mobile office for the mixing and editing of the video that was being shot, so there I would remain in situ for the duration. One thing that amazed me when the show happened is that there was no fencing for crowd control, so soldiers were used to make a human fence. Just rows and rows of soldiers in their uniform being used as a wall; it was surreal.'

Chris Harte, a Transam driver, remembers the event vividly. 'As this was never on the cards when we started the tour, it was all quite unexpected, and it was my first ever trip to Russia. We set off from Barcelona empty and double manned. All of the equipment and three of the trucks were flown in Antonovs directly, while we hot-footed across Europe to collect everything after the show. It went well for us until we got to the border. As soon as we left Poland and got into Russia at Brest, the weather changed, much for the worse. It started raining and would not stop. The daylight was so bleak it was like it was already winter. Couple to this the state of the roads and sure enough disaster struck. There were sixteen trucks heading to Moscow; out of those eight crashed! These ranged from minor damage, including us, to one truck ripping the diesel tank off and being stuck for two weeks! We left the road in exactly the same spot as two other trucks, jackknifing, yet luckily only denting the cab. It was a real hullabaloo getting unstuck, but we managed it and got to Moscow with just about enough time to have a break before the end of the show. It was a real eye-opener!'

Mike parked with David 'Jamie' Jamieson, alongside a Lithuanian Volvo F12. (Mike Ashby)

The 'token photo stop' at the Europe/Asia border. This is situated close to the town of Miass, en route to Chelyabinsk. (Mickey Packham)

Delivering in Nizhny Novgorod, where it plummeted to -38. A consignment of Rover engines for Volga cars delivered by Steve Clark. (Steve Clark)

Steve Makin parked beside a MiG. He was told not to take any photos … (Steve Makin)

On the chain gang. Steve Makin utilising the snow chains to gain traction. (Steve Makin)

En route to Moscow. The Foden was hired by Land Rover for their driver. He had been travelling with the regular Kepstowe drivers and was adamant about being put up in hotels en route. Sadly the smile on his face soon evaporated when they crossed the frontier into Russia! (Steve Makin)

Alan Bremner meeting another British haulier Trevor Starkes on the bleak road towards Moscow. Trevor was working for a different haulier to Kepstowe, but everyone from the same country was a friend on the road in places like this, and there was little animosity. (Trevor Starkes)

Moldova

With Moldova gaining its independence with the fall of the USSR in 1991, it was expected to be part of the CIS group of countries. However, in March 1992, it was officially recognised as an independent state by the United Nations.

The soil that makes up a large part of the country of Moldova is some of the best in the world for growing Chardonnay grapes. In fact, Mileștii Mici is the home of the largest wine cellar in the world. It stretches for 200km, although only 55km is in use, and can hold almost 2 million bottles of wine. This was well known and utilised while part of the Soviet Union. When the union collapsed, the wine-growing areas were generally either destroyed or left to rack and ruin. A few enterprising outsiders already knew the secrets of the soil there, especially some from Australia and France. They were very keen to set about building the area back up and be ready to start exporting to the world again.

Steve Clark had undertaken a delivery to the Ukrainian city of Odessa, and was asked to collect a consignment of wine from the country's capital, Chișinău.

'It was summertime, and really hot and humid. I had managed to get across the border easy enough, just the usual slow-moving queue. About halfway along the route, however, the road was blocked by a machine gun post set up by one of the various factions fighting in the country, with two soldiers who had clearly been imbibing the local tipple. The bridge that had been standing on the road had been blown up. A bulldozer had created a diversion across the fields to take all the traffic into the nearest town, which also had a bridge that would allow everyone to cross the Dnister river and carry on westwards. When I arrived here, there were tanks on either side, in a sort of

Steve Clark at the town of Odessa, Ukraine. (Steve Clark)

The ramshackle Ukraine–Moldova border. (Steve Clark)

Mexican stand-off. It was pretty hair-raising to see. Thankfully it was business as usual and off I trundled along with the other traffic.

'The excitement of the day was not finished, however; before long I got a puncture on my trailer. I was sweating buckets changing the wheel, but I wanted to try and get the collection done as it was Friday and I wanted to get going back towards home. When I arrived at the exporter's I was told the load would not be ready until Monday. Disheartened somewhat, I decided to check into a hotel so I could get a good wash after the day's events. I found one in the city, but when I went to book a room, I was told that I had to have a visa in my passport to do so. Well, I had managed to get this far without one, and they were quite perplexed as to how I had managed it. They made a couple of phone calls, and a little while later, a lady met me at reception. She took me on some local trams and buses to a rather nondescript building, where for twenty dollars I had a visa put into my passport there and then. With me now officially in the country, I was taken back to the hotel, and allowed to book myself a room.

'Come the Sunday, I met a group of Dutch businessmen at the hotel who had just arrived. We got talking and they invited me to join them for dinner at a local restaurant. While we were there, they were telling me their business plans of becoming wine importers using Moldovan wine. When they came to ask me why I was there, I had to tell them that I was collecting a full load of said wine to take to England! This deflated their business idea as I think they thought that no one had tried to fill this gap in the market, but they were a little too late. Unperturbed, we carried on with a few more drinks and some good food, and come the end of the evening, they insisted on paying for everything, and would not have it any other way.'

Richard Warren discovered that corruption was something that was taken seriously in this former Soviet state, much to his surprise.

Nick Reynolds had agreed to help Kepstowe out by loading a trailer with machinery in Liverpool for them. While heading down the M6 towards the London depot, Richard gave him a call. 'I remember Richard starting to talk about "when we get to Ukraine". I stopped him and made it quite clear that I was only helping out and was not shipping out today. He kind of ignored what I was saying and kept banging on about a plan for when we got there. I just let him run on, knowing it was nonsense and I would be at home that night having a beer or two. Well, somehow, and to this day I don't know how they did persuade me, I was shipping out with Richard destined for Kiev! We both had a load of Samsonite suitcases to deliver, quite a regular job. This particular part went as well as could be expected, an easy run across the west, gradually getting worse as we headed east. Soon enough we both had emptied the trailers. After touching base with the office, we were told we had to head across to Moldova to load wine, which was coming back to Sainsbury's at Wimbledon, which would make a nice round trip.'

At the time, Moldova had not long become independent and was recovering from a lot of infighting between various factions struggling for power or independence. Richard takes up the story.

'All along the roads, sometimes not even a mile apart, would be camps of rag-tag soldier-looking types of all ages and varieties. Invariably, they would want some sort of bribe to let us go past, which was just par for the course. We would carry a lot of bootleg CDs with us that we would buy in Poland for such occurrences. With some terrible-quality CD or maybe a tin of corned beef, we would be on our way to the next 'checkpoint' for the next stage of bartering. At the town of Dubăsari there was a bridge that spanned the gorge, which was officially closed due to structural damage it had sustained during the fighting. Some enterprising soldiers had created their own checkpoint and for a fee would allow vehicles over, which would save at least a day's diversion. This was 50 dollars well spent in anyone's book. We paid our 'toll' and crossed the somewhat rickety bridge.'

Eventually the duo arrived at their respective loading sites; Richard was loading at Hîncești and Nick at Cricova. The two towns are around 50km apart. Cricova is remarkable as it has a whole underground 'city' that houses the world's second-largest wine vaults.

The loading of the trailers would end up taking a couple of days in total. The entire operation was done by hand; no forklifts here to speed things up.

Richard recalls: 'I told them the exact border both of us wanted to get out of Moldova back into Ukraine to head home so they could fill out the paperwork for us. When I arrived back at the border, however, I soon realised that my paperwork was written out for exiting into Romania rather than Ukraine. I think despite what I had asked, they assumed that being as I loaded so close to Romania I would want to exit out through there and ignored my request. I know I should have checked myself before I left, but we all make mistakes. The problem was that the Moldovan customs had either not noticed or cared, so I was stamped out and into 'no man's land' by this point, but the Ukrainians would not have it, and would not let me proceed. By now, Nick had already cleared in front of me, and with no mobile phones or satellite phones, I could not get hold of him to let him know my predicament. Initially he wouldn't have thought too much of it as borders would always take hours. Well, I stood my ground and refused to go back. Eventually, a large black Mercedes car appeared as if from nowhere, and your archetypal heavies in black leather jackets extracted themselves from the car. One of them came over, and he spoke a little bit of English. Introducing himself as KGB Moldova, he told me that I would have to go back to Chișinău to have the paperwork amended. I explained that I could not afford to, because every time I wanted to cross the bridge at Dubăsari, it would cost me 50 dollars, so to go there and back would cost me at least 100 dollars, which I did not have any more after having to pay so many bribes in his country. With this I was asked to go with him.

'Well I thought I had said the worst thing possible to him! I was led away by their car to a typical Soviet-style shabby-looking building in the closest local town. I was in there all afternoon repeating my story over and over. More and more people would come in, with more important looking uniforms each time, asking the same things again and again. Eventually the man who I met at the border said to give him 50 dollars. I thought I would give him 1,000 to get the hell out of there at this point. But to my amazement, he took the money and noted down all the serial numbers on the notes. When he gave it back, he told me to pay the bribe, and then pretend I had a problem with my truck and stop. I was taken back to my truck, and I retraced my tyre tracks back to the bridge. I paid my 'toll', luckily they didn't pick up on the sweat on the notes, but then the following KGB men were a bit too quick with their sting operation. They lined up all the soldiers and started screaming at them nose to nose. Whatever was said at one point, all the lower-ranked men stood back, leaving just the sergeant. He had his lapels ripped off, his gun taken away and he was bundled into a van and taken away! The man from the KGB then said to me "you can go now". I pointed out that when I come back, they are going to hang me from this bridge for all this trouble. He smiled, and just said: "You will have no more problems here" and left me to carry on.

'I finally arrived back at the winery, and to say I was fuming would be an understatement. Some of the Australians asked why I was back here, so I let rip with a tirade of words to express my disgruntlement at them getting the paperwork wrong and causing me all these issues. They were somewhat apologetic and set to work getting new paperwork sorted out. The following day when it was all ready, I was then told to go to the border with a Czech-registered truck that was also loading there. I thought, 'This is all I need, some ancient Liaz drawbar (Liaz is an old defunct truck manufacturer from Czechoslovakia) making me take about eight hours longer than needed.' I walked around the corner and saw a nearly new Scania 143 450, which I would have trouble keeping up with!

'We hot-footed it back to the border, over the bridge once again, without any issues as promised, and got ourselves through this time with no real hassles. By now, I was around two days behind Nick at least, and decided to try and make some time up. I drove day and night, not something advisable, and certainly not the night driving part, which was extremely dodgy beyond Poland. I got as far as the town of Lviv, which is the last large town before getting back to the queue for the border with Europe. This was also the site of the last police checkpoint. Naturally I was pulled over, and they decided that the fact my number plate light was blown was a big problem. I was so fed up, I made it known, and pointed out that every truck on the road other than me barely had any lights working, and that I would park there for the night instead if it was such a problem.

'After a night's sleep, which was much needed, I went and joined the queue for Poland. Somehow, and I still have no idea how, I had ended up in front of Nick in the queue! The first we knew of that was when a Russian driver spotted Nick behind me, stopped and tried to tell him I was in front in the queue. Nick was so bewildered at this he actually started walking up the road, and sure enough spotted me. He promptly drove up and joined me, stress free and well rested unlike myself, and we got ourselves back to London to unload without any further issues.'

Steve Tovey and Michael Mudie had two trailers of machinery for a canning factory in Chișinău. Loaded from a closed-down factory in England, the duo set off. First stop was to be Brussels.

'We had to get visas from the consulate for entry. There was no embassy in London at the time, so we had to go to Brussels,' recalls Steve. 'We parked in a Shell garage on the motorway and had to get a taxi into the city centre. We went and presented ourselves, our documents and paperwork and were told it may take a day or two.

'This turned into three days just to get a visa. I remember Michael remarking: "If it is this hard to get a visa then how bad will the border be?" On the third day, we actually woke the man up in the building, he appeared at the door in his dressing gown. I think maybe he had had enough of us by then because that day we finally had the visas in our passports and could get going. Usually, if you look at a map, the best route would be to go via Romania. But for some reason we were told to go via Poland and Ukraine. I think the reasoning was that it was one fewer border crossing to contend with going via Germany, Austria, Hungary and Romania, and the queues involved with this route. But also us drivers knew the route well through Poland, as well as the borders, so we could

The late, great Michael Mudie, awaiting unloading in Chişinău, Moldova. (Steve Tovey)

navigate the maze of customs windows a lot easier than having to learn a new border.'

The drive there went somewhat smoother than the visa fiasco thankfully for the duo, as well as the border crossings. Despite the winter weather and cold, they arrived in February 1999. Upon arrival at the factory, the foreman greeted them. Steve recalls Michael noticing that he was missing a couple of digits on one hand. 'I remember him saying to the chap: "I can see why you need some new machinery" and keeping a straight face. I had to go around the other side of my trailer, so I didn't laugh in this poor guy's face!'

With the machinery offloaded, the pair headed back to Kiev, and collected a load of pipe fittings bound for the UK, a regular return load for Kepstowe at the time.

Mickey Packham also delivered a full load of hospital equipment to Chișinău. This was donated from around the UK, which had been consolidated into Kepstowe's warehouse, loaded into his truck, and off he set.

'I don't remember a huge amount about the particular job, but I do remember it seeming to be such a dark country, by that I mean the lack of street lights. I know most of the USSR seemed that way but Moldova just seemed to have less than anyone. Another hazard was that local criminals had taken to stealing manhole covers to sell for scrap metal, so you really had to have your eyes on the road in the towns as you could do some serious damage dropping a wheel into one of them. The people were quite guarded I would say, not rude, but just suspicious of me and did not come across as overly friendly. But with the country pretty much in the middle of a civil war, I guess it was understandable. There seemed to still be a heavy Russian presence about, which cannot have been helping matters. Upon arrival at the hospital, it really was in need of some help, it had been really neglected. The doctors and nurses here were quite friendly and welcoming, which made a pleasant change. Once I had unloaded all the equipment, I was sent for a collection of wine to return back to the UK.'

Ukraine

Ukraine is now a country well known around the world, sadly for the wrong reasons. From the horrific famine in the 1930s, to the Chernobyl disaster and the invasion by Russia in 2022, this country has been struck blow after blow. The national flag depicts a blue sky over a yellow field of wheat, if you were to drive through, this was pretty much what you would see for miles upon miles. It was known as the bread basket of Europe due to its proficiency in wheat production. Every concrete town sign has a depiction of an ear of wheat by the town's name.

The biggest problems the drivers faced in Ukraine was a lack of familiarity at the borders. As they were regular visitors at the main Russian frontiers, drivers knew the formalities back to front. With Ukraine it almost seemed like arriving there for the first time, every time. This would often lead to crossing times taking longer than the bigger borders.

Richard Warren had to collect some fine art from the Ukrainian equivalent to our National Portrait Gallery in Kiev.

'I was expecting to have people gingerly handling any of these pieces with white gloves on and the utmost care. Of course not, this was not the west, and this wasn't how it was done. I had a Transamerica rental tilt trailer, and they decided the easiest way to load me was to utilise some of the boards from the trailer's superstructure. These were laid down the steps outside, with me reversed up to the steps. They then slid large packing cases with priceless works of art down the boards until they hit the trailer. Then they were manhandled by several bulky men into the trailer. The cases that held the works were just stuffed full of old newspapers and any old rubbish they could find to pack them out. I was taking them back to Edinburgh. When I arrived there, as soon as I was unloaded and had the paperwork signed off, I got out of range as quickly as I could before they started opening the cases up as I had no idea what sort of horrors could be inside them!'

Rod Withers recalls one run for all the wrong reasons, namely all the issues along the way.

'The job was for Mobil Oil, all around the south of the country. I was parked with Danny McAuliffe at the Riders Motel in Poland. Danny had a large generator on his new low-loader, and so we ran together to one of the most southerly Polish borders that trucks can use into Ukraine. With all the customs taken care of, I headed south towards the Crimea region. I had five deliveries, Kherson, Sevastopol, Dnipro, Donetsk and finally Mariupol. Two of the delivery points were quite frankly tiny to get in and out of, I still don't know quite how I managed it without smashing some cars up, but that was some of the fun of it I guess! I had a rental step frame trailer on because the reload was quite large. This was from a town called Tuapse, Russia, not too far through the border. It is on the road towards Sochi and the road hugs the coast of the Black Sea for a lot of the way and it made a lovely drive, much more scenic than what I was used to with the normal Russian trucking. The collection was some ship piston rings going to Rotterdam. I remember I had to wait for the load and the paperwork to be ready in the town's TIR park, so I settled in for a long wait. I had barely got my kettle on when a Turkish truck parked alongside me. He promptly got his trailer's side box open where they store most of their food and invited me for some lunch, which consisted of fresh olives and feta, washed down with some sweet Turkish chai tea. As I did not have a chair to sit on, he even gave me his own one to sit on and he sat on a mat on the floor. The Turks and Iranians are probably some of the most generous drivers on the road.

'The next day everything was ready, so off I went and got the load inside the trailer, secured and ready to go. Chatting with the interpreter who was assisting in the whole operation, he proudly told me how he was earning the equivalent of $100 a week. I did not have the heart to tell him what truck drivers in the west were earning at the time, but like nowadays, it is all relevant to our cost of living.

'It was a short drive back to the Ukraine border, and the Russian customs did not take too long. At this point I jinxed things by thinking: "I might be through and done within a day here", big mistake! The Ukrainians found a problem with the paperwork, which the Russians had either missed or ignored, and there was no way I could get through. Frustrated and annoyed, I had no option but to head back into Russia again. I got in contact with the Kepstowe office in Moscow and it was decided that I should head there and get the paperwork changed and sorted and then head back to Rotterdam through Belarus and Poland. This added a few days onto the trip. With the usual queues and shenanigans getting back into Europe, it was a simple case of get myself to Rotterdam as quickly as I could, get unloaded and head for home and some time off.'

Vince Coventon's first job for Kepstowe was destined for Kiev and then back to Brno in the Czech Republic.

'I was taking a truck on behalf of Unipart from the car plant at Cowley just outside Oxford. There was an exhibition on in the two cities. I was to take the truck and show trailer out, assemble the trailer and then I would have about a week in the city. The trailer is much like the large custom campers you get, which extend out and become a mini showroom. As I had never been as far as East Germany before, this was a real eye-opener for me. The truck itself was a Volvo FL10, which was a lovely truck to drive. However, they were designed with large fleets in mind, and maybe the occasional night out, not several weeks at a time, so the cab was small and severely lacking storage. Every night I would have to empty the bunk of my things into the footwells, across the seats and wherever I could stash it to go to bed.

In the morning, after getting dressed while laid down you had to reverse the process. That was the only real issue with the truck and the job itself. When it came to the actual exhibition, I became a bartender essentially. The main man from Unipart had told me that if anyone who looked important arrived, offer them a drink and get their attention, which I duly did. I had also had some time to look around the city beforehand. It was like nothing I had seen before, such a culture shock of fashion and building styles. The cars that were novelties on UK roads were all that people had there; I lapped it up.

'When the Kiev exhibition was over, it was a case of pack it all away and head back to Brno. I actually flew home from there for a fortnight as the next exhibition would not be taking place until then. Two weeks later I flew back, assembled the trailer once again, became a barman once more, and when it was all done, packed up and took it back to Cowley. I had thoroughly enjoyed it all and had made such a good impression with Unipart that they gave a glowing report back to the office, which cemented my place in the company.'

Azerbaijan

Azerbaijan had been invaded in 1920 by Russia due to its rich oil deposits as Lenin knew they would require these to power Soviet Russia. This brought the country into the USSR. They broke away and became independent a little before the union was dissolved in 1991. Despite the vast majority of the country being Muslim, the country's constitution does not declare an official religion.

Baku or Bust!

Baku, capital of Azerbaijan, would hold a yearly conference and exhibition for the oil and gas industry. Titled the Caspian Oil and Gas Exhibition, it was organised by Spearhead Exhibitions based in London.

The exhibition hall seen from the front. (Steve Tovey)

Parked outside the exhibition hall, Baku. (Mickey Packham)

Unloaded and finished for the time being in Baku. (Steve Clark)

The venue was somewhat unusual; it had been intended to be an ice-skating hall but had never actually opened as such. It was decided instead to turn it into an exhibition centre.

Kepstowe had the exclusive handling rights on the exhibition floor, so would supply the labour and equipment for this to happen. A 20ft container converted to an office was sent on the first trip and left in situ to be used year after year. They would send several trucks at a time to supply the event with everything that was required. The labour would generally be the truck

Needs must to get the trucks unloaded, health and safety optional. (Steve Tovey)

Mickey Packham helping to position a helicopter. (Richard Warren)

drivers, who would be parked in Baku for about a fortnight while it all went on.

The first time this exhibition was held was in 1992. The trucks would depart from the various loading places at the beginning of May. For the first two years, the trucks would drive up to Sweden, catch a ferry to Finland and enter Russia. They would then head to Moscow for any last collections and pick up an armed guard for the next part of the journey. From Moscow they would head south, towards the notorious breakaway region of Dagestan, who were vying for their independence at the time. This caused one or two sleepless nights for all the drivers. Steve Clark has a not so fond memory of the first trip.

Right and below: Before the departure from the Moscow depot. Owner-driver Mick Twemelow's Daf can be seen far right. Chris Everitt's Iveco has its main beam on as Pete Newlyn had been interviewed by the BBC in front of it about driving in Russia. (Steve Clark & Mickey Packham)

Parked for the day. The Mercedes trucks belonged to Central Asia Trans. (Steve Clark)

Convoying south. (Steve Clark)

'I happened to be in Moscow with my own truck on a totally separate job. I was then asked if I would be able to take a different Volvo belonging to another company with the others down to Baku as the driver had lost his nerve and flown home. I agreed, thinking it would be a laugh, and a nice earner getting paid while my truck was not being used. The worst part was not the driving, but the flight from Baku back to Moscow.

'For my flight back, I had paid in US dollars, which meant that I got to go first class. This included such luxuries as a small waiting room, furnished with what looked like old school chairs from the 1950s. Unlike pretty much any other first-class lounge though, there were no refreshments provided. When the flight was called, a very large Azeri woman led us into first class through a mass of humanity all trying to be the first through security. She was just barging people out of the way! She took us out to a Russian-built Tupolev aeroplane. We took our seats at the front of the aircraft, then the rest of the mob piled on filling the rest of the seats. When they were full, they started to fill all the available space on the floor. At least I had a seat belt, even though it didn't work, and I wondered why the people on the floor had so much stuff with them. They had baskets of food and drink, and it soon became apparent why; the in-flight catering was second to none, there simply wasn't any! Russian aircraft design at the time was not brilliant. I tried using the toilet, and after stepping over everyone, I managed to locate it against the far wall of the plane. Being as the fuselage is round, I found it impossible to take a pee standing. Clearly everyone else also had this issue, and I merely added to the lake of urine I was standing in. Finally, after four very long hours, we landed in Moscow. The plane hit the runway and proceeded to bounce down the tarmac. All the overhead lockers flipped open, spilling the contents on to the people below. No wonder they all clapped the flight crew when we got to the terminal. I don't think I have ever been so relieved to get off a flight in my life.'

Steve Clark at the helm of the truck he was asked to take from Moscow. (Steve Clark)

Traversing the Turkish hills. (Steve Clark)

About to cross the Bosphorus bridge, Istanbul. (Steve Clark)

Stopping at the famous Londra camp, Istanbul. Parked here was a fellow British haulier Ralph Davis. (Steve Clark)

Sugar puffs and Fosters lager. Also note the on road repair of the diesel tank strap with a ratchet strap, a case of make do and mend. (Steve Clark)

The route changed in 1995 to go via Turkey and Georgia without starting from Moscow. This was much preferred by everybody, not only for avoiding the Russian roads and Dagestan, but also the route would hug the Black Sea coast and prove to be a beautiful drive. From Turkey, the trucks would enter Georgia and then transit to Azerbaijan.

Heading through the hills of Turkey. (Steve Clark)

The border crossing from Georgia into Azerbaijan. Roly Long's Scania is to be seen on the right. (Alan Douglas)

Alan Douglas's freshly painted Volvo F16 on his debut trip for Kepstowe, seen pausing in the mountains of Turkey en route to Baku, Azerbaijan. (Alan Douglas)

Taking a breather in the hills. One of the Kepstowe Volvos was starting to overheat so a break was taken. (Alan Douglas)

Roly Long's Scania 143 pausing in the hills in Turkey. This would be the only work he undertook for Kepstowe. (Roly Long)

In 1997 there was another slight deviation on the journey, as Steve Clark recalls.

'It was the year we went over the mountains on more of a dirt track than a road, instead of taking the coastal route like previous years. The mountain pass of Bolu was well travelled by the Middle East veterans of which Kepstowe now had a few. They knew some good places to stop for a coffee or a beer. This route brought us out at the coast at the town of Samsun. Although we were not meant to be on this route as it was off the designated TIR route, we were also not really meant to be on the coast road either as it was not for transiting traffic. We took it because it was shorter, and we luckily never had any trouble from any authorities. I remember there also being a small contingent from another company who tagged along with us, who were also en route to Baku. They were working for an American company who were dealing with the Anglo American Oil Company, who had a large depot to the south of Baku.

Hazards of the road. This Turkish haulier has clearly lost his load somehow. (Alan Douglas)

Parked and waiting in the Ulusoy depot at Trabzon, Turkey. (Steve Clark)

The usual driving standards prevail. Meeting a bus that is being undertaken on a hairpin bend is never a good thing. And note the state of the trailer in front of Alan and its load and how it is held on. (Alan Douglas)

'They got permission for us all to park there so we could get showered and fed. I even got their dentist to sort my toothache out for me, which had been a real pain since Istanbul. That was one heck of a relief!

'I remember that a truck from the other company lost its 20ft container near the town of Ganja, Azerbaijan. Quite how this happened, I have no idea! They had to find a crane to get it lifted back on. The container was

Traversing small Turkish towns. (Alan Douglas)

heading to the same exhibition as us, and when it was unloaded at the site compound everything inside was covered in paint!'

Upon arrival at the coastal town of Trabzon, all the drivers had to park at the huge Turkish haulier Ulusoy's yard and get their visas arranged for Georgia and Azerbaijan. This process took a day, which forced the drivers to have to retreat to a bar and test how the Turkish beers tasted. Once the visas had been obtained, it was onwards to the border town of Sarpi, and into Georgia.

Below and opposite: A fellow British company's misfortune of losing a container on the road somehow. With the help from the Kepstowe drivers and office, a local crane was arranged for reloading. (Steve Clark)

SHAH DENIZ
BAKU

A crew photo with some local Azeri workers. (Steve Clark)

Queueing at the Georgian border on the way home from another successful exhibition. The ramshackle hut to the right is the actual border post and customs office. The red Iveco is a Finnish sub-contractor, Ese Mäkinen. (Steve Clark)

Sub-contractor Roland 'Roly' Long undertook his only job for Kepstowe this year. He first loaded in London, and then onto Milan to finishing loading on 6 May. He met up with the other drivers at the famous Londra camp located near Istanbul before they headed east. 'It was a beautiful drive along the coast, lots of tea plantations, but not many flat surfaces due to the ravages of the weather. When the sun went behind the clouds, it could look like a really forbidding area.' He remembers the border crossing from Turkey into Georgia vividly. 'There was a huge pair of iron gates built into the rock there, it was a daunting sight.' As with all the others, after reloading the same equipment, he finished unloading in London on 26 June.

An exhibition which that stood out in Beth King's memory was her first job 'on site'. With about a dozen trucks en route, she had to arrange all the drivers' visas first in London, and then fly out to meet them at the port of Ancona in Italy before they boarded the ferry to Greece. 'The next time I would see all the drivers was when I was helping with arranging the customs clearance at the Turkish–Georgian border. The trucks were placed onto a transit under bond to the exhibition grounds in Azerbaijan where the unloading was happening (meaning duty did not have to be paid as the loads were not being bought / sold, as they would be returned after the exhibitions). My job was to be the site co-ordinator, to make sure the trucks were unloaded as needed and arrange where and how the exhibition itself was set up. Of course, the local customs agent would always want some sort of 'gift' to make them do their job of actually clearing the trucks, things like a pen or a hat, so I had to have a bag full of these sorts of 'gifts' to ease the process.

Igor from the Moscow office was providing assistance to the trucks en route to Baku. In the photo are Roly Long and Richard Warren's Scanias and Alan Douglas's Volvo. Paul Saunders can also be seen in the baseball cap to the right. (Alan Douglas)

Beth King having some breakfast in Chris Everitt's Iveco. (Steve Tovey)

'One downside to the job was the hotels that we used to have to stay in, run by Intourist. I use the term hotel very loosely, however. It was potluck if you would get hot water, brown water or even any water to your room. You could be stood at the bar and watch rats running about, which would put you off your food somewhat. These were not even a budget hotel, they cost a fortune even by British standards at the time!'

Mickey Packham loved these trips. 'I did seven or eight trips, and I loved them all. Not just for the sitting around the pool sipping a cold beer in the sunshine, honest! No, the overall atmosphere was just great, it really was a laugh a minute. It was probably the closest I have been to having a holiday at work, just real good fun with a good bunch of friends. I looked forward to them happening every year.'

In 1998 the route changed back to the original trek down through Russia. It would remain the chosen path for the next few years. The situation had eased towards the south of the country, and it was deemed safe enough for the trucks to travel this way. The last year the company was involved was 2001, with only Dave Button and Pete Newlyn going overland. The rest of the loads were undertaken by Turkish trucks, a sign of the changing times.

'I remember it well,' says Dave. 'We were told we could get visas for Georgia at the border, so off we set for Turkey. This time, however, we stuck to the official TIR route across the mountains, no beach resorts this time. Once we had exited Turkey, we soon found out that we could not get a visa at the border with Georgia. The only thing for it was for me to take

With the downtime, the drivers explored the ancient part of Baku. (Steve Tovey)

Everyone chipping in to get the trucks unloaded. John Mantle is facing the camera holding part of the exhibition stand. (Steve Clark)

Parked outside the Hotel Absheron, Baku. (Mickey Packham)

A detour around the town of Grozny, Chechnya. (Alan King)

both of our passports back to a Georgian embassy and get these arranged. After a night in the truck, I got myself up early in the morning, as I knew it would be a long, arduous bus trip ahead of me, not your National Express type that was for sure. I left Pete in no man's land with the trucks and headed back to the Turkish side.

'Once I explained the issue to the border guards, they happily waved me through to go and resolve this. Being as there is a lot of foot traffic coming through and heading for the town of Trabzon, finding a bus heading that way was not a problem. However, this foot traffic was carrying literally anything they had to sell, be it food, pots or pans, or livestock like goats and sheep. Therefore, the bus I managed to find was rammed with mainly women and goats! The other problem was, despite me being a driver, I get travel sick. This was not an ideal situation, to put it lightly. Luckily, however, I was somewhat of a novelty on board, and all the women wanted to mother me and tend to me, and their livestock of course! This somewhat long bus journey got me to the embassy, and so once the visas were obtained, I was back on a bus, luckily without livestock this time, and heading back to the border in the same day to be reunited with Pete and my truck. I had not been so relieved to have my own cab and its peace and quiet in a long, long time.'

In 1998, Alan Johnson and four other trucks were all contracted to load in Berlin for Ganja, Azerbaijan. There were another six to go afterwards too, which were taken by various other drivers. Alan was to utilise his low-loader for the main load, and the other trucks were taking the ancillary equipment. One of Dave Hogg's trucks in his company Hogspeed, another well-known name in long-distance transport, was sub-contracted in, driven by Bob May, along with owner-operators

Nigel Harness supervising the loading of his trailer in Germany. (Alan Johnson)

Alan Johnson with his low-loader. (Alan Johnson)

Seddon Atkinson Strato owned by sub-contractor Robert Cantrill, a slightly more unusual truck on the roads doing long distance at the time. (Alan Johnson)

Nigel Harness, Robert Cantrill and Ted Harris. Ted's truck was driven by a man called Dave Sadler. Ted had bought Alan Douglas's F16 when he had bought a newer Volvo FH12.

Alan takes up the story. 'This was quite an urgent rush job, certainly not what you would usually get with Kepstowe, so I guess that the customer had been let down at the last minute by someone and so they stepped in. The machine I was loading weighed in at around 50 tonnes, so it would need movement permits and so on. When I spoke with the office, they told me there was only a permit from the Finnish border to Moscow, did I think I could get it through! I knew that if the proverbial hit the fan they would cover the costs, and so I said I would give it a go.

'We loaded on a Saturday, and I was heading to Lübeck to catch the ferry to Finland, which would take me to the correct border for the one permit that we had. Being a Saturday was a double-edged sword, there were fewer trucks on the road, which meant fewer enforcement vehicles were about, but the chances of getting stopped and inspected were increased with fewer trucks about. I got up and into the docks late on the Saturday night and blew a sigh of relief! My ferry was not until Monday morning, so a leisurely day on the Sunday was had pottering about and relaxing.

'When I woke up Monday, I opened my curtains to see the BAG had set up a checkpoint right in front of my truck, checking trucks entering the docks! (The BAG is the German equivalent to the British DVSA, but with a much more stringent reputation.) I thought, I do not need this, I will have a cup of tea and just see what happens. With my brew drank, I chose my time to fire the truck up and head for the shipping lanes; no one batted me an eyelid! Another breath of relief was blown, and I booked on the ferry and sailed to Finland. Upon arrival at the Russian border, there was the usual farce, although this time they thought they would really extract some money out of me with the load being so heavy. But I knew I had a permit, I stuck to my guns, and begrudgingly they eventually cleared me, and I was on my way. I travelled down to Moscow to the Kepstowe office and met up with the other trucks who had gone overland through Poland.

'We set off south in no particular hurry as the roads and my load dictated this. There is a long stretch somewhere along the road south when you run parallel with a railway line. At some point you cross over it at a level crossing and carry on south on the other side. There is a stop sign to check for trains, however no one ever does. As we were approaching the crossing, there was a Lada in front of me, and I knew they would not bother stopping. I had a set of train horns fitted to my truck, which I had bought many years previously in Turkey, and so I decided to give him a blast just as he was about to cross over. You have never seen a car stop so quickly! However, once over a little further down the road I got my karma for this trick. The police stopped us all, checked our tachographs, which clearly showed none of us had stopped, and promptly fined us all for not stopping at the stop sign.

'Traversing the small region of Kalmykia, at a police point it was decided that they wanted to weigh my truck, just what I did not need with no permits. The weighbridge was on the other side of the road, however, so they wanted me to turn around and get weighed. Here I saw my opportunity. With my worst driving skills, I managed to get my reversing totally wrong time and time again, totally blocking the road. Eventually they got so fed up with this

Another day, another break for refreshments from the trailer box. (Alan Johnson)

Coffee time, somewhere in the middle of nowhere. (Alan Johnson)

palaver they told me just to go! We knew that next we would get close to Chechnya, but that we would skirt around on an unofficial diversion. Unsurprisingly, no one was keen to actually take the shorter route through the disputed region. Keeping close to the coast of the Caspian Sea, it was a nice, warm and scenic drive. The border point at Samur was as average as a Russian border point could be, and we made our way to Baku, where Kepstowe had set up another office. Former driver Matt Towse was running this part of the business, it was mainly for the regular oil and gas exhibitions that we served. From Baku we headed to the site for offloading.

Almost a Turkish barbers! Bob May giving Robert Cantrill a spruce up in a TIR park. (Alan Johnson)

Alan Johnson's was probably the easiest offload. Simply remove the tractor unit from the trailer and drive the machine off. (Alan Johnson)

The German crew arrived shortly after we did, dressed in their best clothes, which seemed odd for site work. It turned out that someone along the way had stolen all their luggage from the flight and so they only had the clothes they stood in!'

Georgia

This was one of the lesser-visited countries. Most years it would be transited by the trucks heading for Baku, however a few deliveries did happen, but they were only to the capital, Tbilisi. Being a small and impoverished state, there is little industry and the country is mostly farmland, with little trade with the west.

Vince Coventon undertook quite a journey in a day-cabbed Volvo FL7. 'It was a reconditioned fuel tanker which was to be used at the airport in Tbilisi. Therefore, there would be no need for it to be equipped with a sleeper cab as it would not be leaving the airport once it was there. I collected it from Chessington and set off. It was also a different overland route rather than a trek across Russia. I was heading for Bulgaria, and so it was down through France, then due to the low weight of the truck I could transit Switzerland, saving some time and also getting some lovely views as well. Dropping into Italy, I headed for Ancona to catch a boat to Greece. This is where the problems began.

'I had a certificate with me to state that the tank had been completely purged of any fuel fumes, so it would not be covered by ADR rules on the road or at sea. However, according to the powers that be, they needed it to be in Italian. After several phone calls back and forth, someone was found in Milan who could arrange this.

It took him two days to arrive at the port. When it was presented, they did a 'test' of the air in the tank. I am sure this was just to be seen to actually be doing something to justify my delay and there was no actual science in their test. With this, they were happy, and so I could board the next ferry.

'Upon disembarking in Patras, I had a lovely drive across Greece, lots of great weather and food. Usually, this is the point where Middle East drivers head into Turkey, as did the Kepstowe trucks heading for Baku for the exhibitions. For this trip I was catching a ferry from Burgas, Bulgaria, direct to Georgia to the port town of Poti. This saved not only transiting Turkey and the costs involved, but also two border crossings, especially as they are not known for their speed in clearing trucks. Due to my delays in Italy, I went hammer and tongs to get to the port. With only two sailings a week, one on a Tuesday and one on Friday, I did not want to lose any more time. I had been told I had to be there by 6pm Friday to ensure getting on board. I managed to arrive at 5pm, only to be told the crossing had been cancelled! A wait of four days was forced upon me. It was pointless trying to go overland and ignore the sailing as the queue from Greece into Turkey could easily cost a couple of days of time. I finally got aboard on Tuesday, and we sailed off across the Black Sea. The ferry crossing took three days, and I made the most of having an actual bunk to sleep in. Sleeping across the seats in the truck certainly was not a lot of fun, especially for two weeks.

'After we had disembarked in Poti, customs were not too much bother, and I got myself to Tbilisi airport. It had taken me about three weeks in total to get there, and originally the office had thought it would be possible in ten to twelve days. If everything had gone right this probably would have been the case, but this led onto the biggest problem of the trip. I was flying home, and there was a flight direct to Heathrow with British Airways from Tbilisi. However, Kepstowe had already pre-booked my flights with Aeroflot. The route was fly to Moscow, and connect with a flight for the UK. Because I had been delayed in the truck, my Russian visa for this trip had expired. At Moscow's Sheremetyevo airport, there are two large terminals. One for internal flights, and one for international routes. To get between the two means you must enter Russian territory as they are not linked. This means you must go through passport control, immigration, etc. The anomaly was that Georgia, despite being a separate country, had its flights still going into the internal flight terminal due to it being part of the old Soviet Union. With an expired visa, however, this was a problem. I was arrested and held in a detention centre overnight. I tried to explain what had happened, but I knew it was a waste of my breath; I had dealt with Russian bureaucracy for long enough at this point. The following day, I was deported back home to Heathrow.'

Kazakhstan

This country is a vast expanse of a whole lot of nothing; it is the world's largest landlocked country, and the ninth largest in the world. Despite its size, its population density is one of the lowest in the world, averaging fewer than six people per square kilometre. Around one third of the territory is known as the Steppe. This stretches for hundreds of miles, containing a few sparse settlements and grassland as far as the eye can see. The road network, should it be called that, consists of tracks with the occasional tarmac, which is seldom looked after, and often rougher than driving on the grass verge to the side of it. It is a land of extreme temperatures, blistering heat in the summer months and cold beyond anything you are likely to experience in the depths of winter. The winds blow unimpeded across the land, and regularly plummets the air to -40 degrees. Almaty was the capital city until 1997, when this changed to Astana. It was also the last of the Soviet states to declare its independence.

Coffee stop to take in the local wildlife. (Dave Button)

Steve Clark and on the right another driver named Steve Holding. 'Are we on the right track do you think?' (Steve Tovey)

Steve Makin arriving at Almaty to deliver on behalf of Kodak. (Steve Makin)

Due to its scarcity of people, facilities such as truck stops and roadside garages were also few and far between, especially when you left the outskirts of whichever town you happened to be passing. Another issue would be that often the garages would often not have any diesel. This created a lot of opportunity for locals with anything big enough to sell diesel from. Ranging from a few jerry cans from the boot of a car to small tanker trucks with a fuel nozzle, drivers would seldom pass these. 'The key was to never let it get too low before you start looking for your next supplier. The small trucks could be very sporadic, so it was usually worth a stop. I even bought some diesel from a train once!' Steve Clark remembers. 'The quality of this roadside fuel could be a little dubious, but what other choice did we have? Besides this, during the harsh winter months, a little petrol would often be mixed in to try and stop the diesel fuel waxing, which leads to engine stalls and then crucially, no hot fans or night heater.'

Dave Button has always been a fan of doing the longer jobs, and a job with Kepstowe certainly kept that appetite whetted. 'I undertook a run out to Almaty in Kazakhstan, which was a regular destination for us. I was delivering a simulator, quite an expensive piece of equipment, and one I was a little concerned whether it would arrive undamaged given the roads to get it out there. The one advantage with it, however, was the entire load did not weigh 5 tonnes, so the truck did not burn as much fuel, and any hills I encountered did not bother it either so I could make good progress.

A great example of a Kazakhstan transport cafe….. (Alan Douglas)

In the middle of nowhere, as usual, was this improvised transport cafe. After parking for the night the duo arrived and prepared breakfast for the hungry drivers. (Steve Clark)

Danny with a Mercedes from Central Asia Trans, both having taken on fuel. (Danny McAuliffe)

Your typical Kazakh refuel. Find a bank and let gravity assist you. (Steve Clark)

'Leaving the UK on 3 July 1998, I was shipped directly into Finland, where I arrived on the 7th. From this border I was in Moscow late on the 8th. The drive onwards was the usual fare, and I was into Kazakhstan on the 12th and then heading to the capital. Upon arrival at the delivery point, to unload it, I was backed up to a set of steps, and it was dragged out of the back of the trailer on some planks of wood. I stood and watched from afar as I did not want to be held responsible if anything went wrong, which it looked like it could at any moment! It was a small miracle really that it had arrived there in one piece with the pounding of the road, although the air suspension all round on truck and trailer certainly helped with that. But even

Delivering a simulator to Almaty. (Dave Button)

more so with their careless unloading. I know sometimes you cannot easily get a forklift, but they were expecting this, and you would have thought someone may have thought about how to unload it with a little more care.

'Once I was empty there, I headed back to Moscow and arrived there on the 23rd. After a couple of days off to have a legally required break, I was loaded with equipment for one of the Russian ballets, which was performing in Monaco. From the impoverished in the east to the overt wealth of Monte Carlo was such a contrast. En route, in France close to Lyon, I was stopped and fined by the French police for driving on Black Saturday. This was a new one on me, also judging by the countless other trucks

Monaco, not your usual delivery address for a truck this size, however with a Russian ballet's equipment from Moscow on board, Dave Button found himself mingling with the rich and famous at Jimmy'z night club. (Dave Button)

LETTRE DE VOITURE INTERNATIONALE (CMR) **INTERNATIONAL CONSIGNMENT NOTE**

SF

COPY 1 SENDER
COPY 2 CONSIGNEE
COPY 3 CARRIER

1 Sender (Name, Address, Country) Expéditeur (Nom, Adresse, Pays) THE SMILING LION COMPANY TEMPLE HOUSE HOOF LANE LONDON NW11 7NE	2 Customs Reference/Status Référence/désignation pour mise en douane 3 Senders/Agents Reference Référence de l'expéditeur/de l'agent EKX/021958
4 Consignee (Name, Address, Country) Destinataire (Nom, Adresse, Pays) EUROCOMFORT FIRM STR DOSTYK 42, APT 45 ALMATY 480100 KAZAKHSTAN	5 Carrier (Name, Address, Country) Transporteur (Nom, Adresse, Pays) KEPSTOWE FREIGHT SERVICES LTD
6 Place & date of taking over the goods (place, country, date) Lieu et date de la prise en charge des marchandises (Lieu, pays, date) EAST MOLESEY, SURREY United Kingdom 03/07/1998	7 Successive Carriers Transporteurs successifs
8 Place designated for delivery of goods (place, country) Lieu prévu pour la livraison des marchandises (lieu, pays) ALMATY KAZAKHSTAN	This carriage is subject, notwithstanding any clause to the contrary to the Convention on the Contract for the International Carriage of Goods by Road (CMR) Ce transport est soumis nonobstant toute clause contraire à la Convention Relative au Contrat de Transport International de Marchandises par Route (CMR)

9 Marks & Nos; No. & Kind of Packages; Description of Goods* Marques et Nos, No et nature des colis, Désignation des marchandises*	10 Gross weight (kg) Poids Brut (kg)	11 Volume (m³) Cubage (m³)
EUROCOMFORT FIRM 1 PIECE ALMATY SRV ENTERTAINMENT SIMULATOR, TEL: (3272)610951 PROGRAMMES & SPARES MR O. FEDOROV (95080000) Unit No: AH 368169	4535	

Carriage Charges Prix de transport DELIVERED DUTY UNPAID	12 Senders Instructions for Customs, etc. Instructions de l'Expéditeur (optional) TIR CARNET: 21370872
Reservations Réserves	14 Document attached Documents Annexés (optional) INVOICES Special agreements Conventions particulières (optional)
Goods Received/Marchandises Reçues	17 Signature of Carrier/Signature du transporteur KEPSTOWE FREIGHT SERVICES LTD 18 Company completing this note Société émettrice KEPSTOWE FREIGHT SERVICES Place and Date; Signature Lieu et date; Signature EAST MOLESEY KT8 03/07/1998

Approved by FTA/RHA/SITPRO UK 1991

730

Left and overleaf: Dave's CMR delivery notes for the round trip. (Dave Button)

parked by the police at the péage (toll booths on the motorway system), to a lot of others as well. They must have made a fortune that day out of us truckers at 600 francs each!

I arrived at Jimmy'z Nightclub in Monaco, and I had to park outside for several days. They were decidedly unimpressed with this; a truck really does lower the tone there among the Ferraris and Lamborghinis after all. I was out of options, as were the club

LETTRE DE VOITURE INTERNATIONALE (CMR) **INTERNATIONAL CONSIGNMENT NOTE**

SF

COPY 2 CONSIGNEE
COPY 3 CARRIER

1 Sender (Name, Address, Country) Expéditeur (Nom, Addresse, Pays)

GOSYDARSTVEN AKAD. THEATRE
IGOR MOISEEV
103050, MOSCOW, TVERSKAY ST 31

2 Customs Reference/Status Référence/désignation pour mise en douane

3 Senders/Agents Reference Référence de l'expéditeur/de l'agent

ME 2660

4 Consignee (Name, Address, Country) Destinaire (Nom, Addresse, Pays)

GONDARD c/o UNIVERSAL AIR
CARGO AEROPORT NICE COTE D AZUR
ZONE DE FRET
NICE FRANCE

5 Carrier (Name, Address, Country) Transporteur (Nom, Addresse, Pays)

KEPSTOWE FREIGHT SERVICES LTD.
UNIT E, IMBER COURT TRADING ESTATE
ORCHARD LANE
EAST MOLESEY
SURREY KT8 OBY
TEL: 0181 - 783 2000
V.A.T. No. 235 7868 26

6 Place & date of taking over the goods (place, country, date) Lieu et date de la prise en charge des marchandises (Lieu, pays, date)

MOSCOW
RUSSIA

7 Successive Carriers Transporteurs successifs

8 Place designated for delivery of goods (place, country) Lieu prévu pour la livraison des marchandises (lieu, pays)

NICE FRANCE

This carriage is subject, notwithstanding any clause to the contrary to the Convention on the Contract for the International Carriage of Goods by Road (CMR)
Ce transport est soumis nonobstant toute clause contraire à la Convention Relative au Contrat de Transport International de Marchandises par Route (CMR)

9 Marks & Nos; No. & Kind of Packages; Description of Goods* Marques et Nos, No et nature des colis, Désignation des marchandises*	**10** Gross weight (kg) Poids Brut (kg)	**11** Volume (m³) Cubage (m³)
54 COLLI THEATRE DECORATIONS	2700,-	

ГРУЗ

12 Carriage Charges Prix de transport

13 Senders Instructions for Customs, etc... Instructions de l'Expéditeur (optional)

ГТД - 05844/24.07.8/0005693

14 Reservations Reserves

МОСКОВСКАЯ СЕВЕРНАЯ ТАМОЖНЯ 05800
ГТК РОССИИ 023
ВЫПУСК РАЗРЕШЕН
Инспектор
«27» 07 1998 г.

15 Document attached Documents Annexés (optional)

16 Special agreements Conventions particulières (optional)

023

17 Goods Received / Marchandises Recues

МИНИСТЕРСТВО КУЛЬТУРЫ РОССИЙСКОЙ ФЕДЕРАЦИИ
УЧРЕЖДЕНИЕ КУЛЬТУРЫ
ГОСУДАРСТВЕННЫЙ АКАДЕМИЧЕСКИЙ АНСАМБЛЬ НАРОДНОГО ТАНЦА ПОД РУКОВОДСТВОМ ИГОРЯ МОИСЕЕВА
МОСКВА

27.07.98

18 Signature of carrier Signature du transporteur

KEPSTOWE FREIGHT SERVICES LTD.
UNIT E, IMBER COURT TRADING ESTATE
ORCHARD LANE
EAST MOLESEY
SURREY KT8 OBY
TEL: 0181 - 783 2000
V.A.T. No. 235 7868 26

19 Company completing this note Société émettrice

20 Place and Date; Signature Lieu et date; Signature

730

SYSTEMFORMS 0171 796 9666 (8.90)

owners as there was not enough room to unload everything. I had to sit and wait for someone to come up with a solution. With everything eventually offloaded there safe and sound, I had a short drive across the coast into Italy, and reloaded from two collection points in Milan before heading back to the UK, arriving back and delivering this last reload on 6 August.'

Almaty Oil and Gas Expo

This series of exhibitions were the same as their Baku counterparts, yet from a truck-driving point of view they were slightly different. The main reason was that the former global forwarder Danzas had the on-site contract for the logistics. (Danzas are now part of DHL Deutsche Post group.)

L–R: Dave Button, Graham Mitchell, Matt Towse, Peter King, John Mantle, David Lloyd and Steve Clark. They were all heading for Almaty to reload from the oil and gas exhibition. Steve's Daf was on its first trip under his ownership, having delivered to a beer bottling plant in Omsk, Russia, beforehand. (Steve Clark)

Convoying towards Almaty. (Steve Clark)

This gave the drivers a lot more time off when they arrived on site because it was not part of their job to help, unlike in Baku. As relationships had been formed with the same stand owners with previous exhibitions, more often than not they would get asked to lend a hand for a few pounds, cash in hand. At times, even the Danzas co-ordinator would ask them for their assistance. Not only would it help with some money for a post-work beer, but it would also help pass the time.

Alan Douglas remembers one trip fondly. 'We had arrived at the Russian–Kazakh border to the east of Kurgan, and the queue was really big. As this was quite time critical, we did not have two or three days to sit about. A couple of us took a walk down to the border to have a chat with the guards. After a little negotiation, and a backhander of 100USD per truck, they would send an armed guard to escort us around this queue of trucks. The guard was essential to save getting projectiles aimed at us by disgruntled queueing drivers!

'When we were in the compound, I made sure that all the trucks got cleared prior to me before I handed any money over. Just like that, within a couple of hours of us having a little chat, we were clear and at the Kazakhstan side. International chatter between drivers is far quicker than any media source in the world, and the guards believed that all their Christmases had come at once. They started talking about money before our feet were on the ground out of the cabs to process our paperwork! Despite the language barrier, we managed to make them understand that holding us up was not a problem at all, if it takes a week, then it takes a week. However, the exhibition we were heading for was being opened by the president himself, so if they wanted to explain to him why this was not going ahead because they would not process us then they could be our guests. Once this realisation sunk in, the rubber stamps were bouncing off the sheets of paper double quick. With us free from customs, we made our way to Almaty, and arrived with a little time to spare, something which would not have happened if we had been stuck in the queue.'

Steve Clark parked for the day in the safety of a police post. (Steve Clark)

Old versus new. Brand new Volvo FH en route to the brand new Volvo dealership and its official launch. (Danny McAuliffe)

With the obligatory camel, taken somewhere on the steppe en route to Almaty. (Danny McAuliffe)

Danny McAuliffe took a brand new Volvo FH tractor unit and show trailer to Almaty. 'It was 1994, when the FH was being launched to replace the successful F series of trucks. My father was living in Almaty at the time and overseeing the set-up of the Volvo dealership for the country. None of Volvo's own demonstrator drivers would entertain the idea of taking a truck that far, so I presume that is how I ended up going. I went out to Gothenburg in my own truck and left it at Volvo's factory. From Sweden, I caught a ferry to Turku, and then the well-trodden Kepstowe path down through the Finnish border to Moscow. From there it was east to Samara, and onwards to the usual border at Petropavl. Once through it was to Karagandy Province and further south to Almaty. All in all, it was around 4,000km from Moscow alone. The truck itself was lovely, being brand new, of course but the trailer was another matter, and a real contrast to the tractor unit. For the unforgiving roads east of Finland, ideally you want something strong and well built. This single-axle, steel suspension relic may have been at some point, but by then it was certainly past its prime, let's just say! It took quite a bit of nursing to keep it going all the way down there.

'Once I was on site, some technicians from Volvo were flown out to take the data from the on-board computers, which was a technology they were developing at the time. As expected, there had not been any problems with the truck; I had been armed with a host of spares, ECUs, etc, however, I did not need any of them. The tractor unit was exhibited at the new dealership and was promptly snapped up by someone. I was flown back to Sweden to collect my own truck and head for a reload and for home. The show trailer was subsequently collected by a Central Asia Trans tractor unit, who had a depot in Almaty, and taken back to Moscow. When it arrived there, Richard Warren had been asked to wait for the truck so he could run with them as their drivers had never been west before. No sooner had they set off west, the first police checkpoint soon hauled the duo in, and the problems began.

'When the police had a look around, they soon noticed that customs had sealed the wrong trailer door, which we were told was a 'big, big problem' of course! They were insisting that the trailer would have to go all the way back to Almaty to be sealed correctly. Fortunately for us, we invited them to have a look inside the trailer, in case there was anything that would sate their request. They were soon happy enough with several Volvo pens, hats, etc that were gifted from the trailer. To be honest, it looked like a bomb had gone off in the back after the pounding the roads had given it. The office furniture was all over the place and damaged, the ceiling had come down, almost everything inside was broken. With their new-found 'gifts' they permitted us to carry on west.

'We made it back into Poland and then to Germany, and the poor driver was terrified of the German police because his truck was somewhat beaten up. We found a Mercedes truck dealer and soon got his minor problems sorted out to ease his nerves. He could not believe the road network; this sort of infrastructure was completely alien to him. We got to Kiel docks so he could drop the trailer and park there for the night. I took him to a local supermarket and once again the cultural differences were staggering for him. Just being able to wander into a supermarket, pick up what takes your fancy from the shelves and pay for it was something we took for granted, but was like a dream to this chap. From Kiel we both went to Rotterdam; he was collecting another trailer for the oil and gas exhibition in Almaty while I was heading back to England.'

The worldwide company De la Rue had a contract to supply the Kazakhstan government a purpose-built plant to enable them to print their own currency. Kepstowe had eight loads one year to deliver. The contract stipulated that the trucks would go to Moscow, and then take an armed guard with the driver onwards; not something any driver wanted, but that was the conditon of the job. John Mante takes up the story.

'My delivery happened in midwinter, so from the moment I crossed the border from Poland it was snow and ice all the way down. While trudging through the winter weather towards Almaty, I was informed of a possible backload via the Inmarsat somewhere inside Kazakhstan. I got th e truck unloaded easy enough and with no trouble; that was one of the advantages of dealing with a company like De La Rue. Then the backload was confirmed to me. It was from the mining town of Ust-Kamenogorsk, to the east of the country, and certainly not en route back home. My armed guard didn't like the sound of the backload, so he phoned his boss in Moscow thinking they would fly him home. Not a chance he was told, and the reason soon became apparent. I set off east with 1,100km to go with one very disgruntled passenger. The landscape became really desolate, almost like the surface of the moon. The reload was 5 tonnes of rare metals, which were used in special steel production. The value was astronomical, tens of millions of US dollars we were told. The knock-on effect of this was that the consignment would be too valuable to transit Poland with their insurance limits. This meant it was back to Moscow to drop my passenger off, and finally get the truck back to myself. Then head west back into Finland.

'It ended up taking me three days to get out of Russia. The customs needed confirmation of the export licence from the Kazakh company before they cleared me. Once I was back in Europe I was heading for the ferry. However, the load was going to Rotterdam, so no cruise on the M/V *Garden* this time. Instead it was a ferry to Sweden before heading south overland through Denmark and Germany before arriving at Rotterdam. I remember I got stopped by a Swedish transport ministry check. The truck was filthy so it was no great surprise; after all the thinking in most countries for some reason is that a dirty truck is one that is not as well maintained as a clean one. After their initial checks yielded nothing untoward, they decided they wanted to inspect the security of the load. I told them it was under TIR conditions and customs sealed, therefore they would need to get customs to break this seal, with no exceptions. Hearing this, and then checking the seal, they soon gave up that idea and let me get on my way. I still had a trailer belly tank full of Russian diesel that they had not picked up on. When I arrived in Rotterdam, the load was soon offloaded and I could breathe a sigh of relief. When you have such expensive loads under your care it can be quite concerning and you have to think a little more and be a little more vigilant.'

Turkmenistan

This is one country to which few drivers from the west have ventured. John Mantle, Dave Button and Steve Tovey all took exhibition equipment in consecutive years, once again for the oil and gas exhibitions that were being held in the capital city of Ashgabat. Rather than go overland, however, both Dave and John caught a ferry from Baku and crossed the Caspian Sea, as Dave recalls.

'In 1999, I had a consignment loaded for the exhibition, and so off I set. The route I was given took me into Russia from Europe and southwards towards Azerbaijan to get the ferry from Baku. I spent an awful night stuck on the border between the region of Dagestan, Russia and Azerbaijan. There were a lot of dubious-looking people lurking around; although I was not frightened, it put me on edge, and it was safe to say I was glad to see daylight appear. Afterwards I thought to myself, "Well that is just another night at a Russian border with no sleep!"

'Once at Baku, I found the ferry to take me across the Caspian Sea. I thought it would get a bit better. How wrong I was! Without exaggerating, this is probably the worst ferry crossing I have ever taken in my life, and I have had some bad crossings. It is a train ferry, so I was loaded in among some train carriages for the crossing. There were no cabins for the duration, but for a handful of dollars I bought the chief engineer's cabin to use. There was no restaurant and much of the passenger lounge was fire damaged that had not been remedied so it was out of bounds. We also spent more of our time drifting than under steam due to the constant breakdowns the boat suffered. After two days of this debacle of a crossing we arrived in Turkmenbashi. I could not wait to get off this floating disaster, but there was still one more surprise waiting for me. For the disembarkation process, they needed two trains and there was only one working train. On other routes this wouldn't normally be a problem, however, they needed two for balance purposes on this boat, so when they tried to remove the carriages, the ferry actually started to tip over. I do not think I have ever been so pleased to drive off a ferry in my life! Once I was safely back on solid ground, I hit the road for the expo at Ashgabat. It was fair to say I was not looking forward to the return journey one bit!'

John Mantle had the longest trip of the trio. After unloading his exhibition equipment, he then had to carry on across to Almaty and deliver a consignment before returning back to the exhibition site to reload before heading home.

'It was 1997. I loaded my truck from London and then I went to Italy to complete the loading. When this was done and the trailer sealed, I went south to the port of Brindisi and shipped across to Patras in Greece. Then it was the old Middle East route I knew from my Pro-Motor days into Turkey and across the Bosphorus, but then head for Georgia and not Arabia. Transiting Georgia to Baku,

Dave Button's truck tucked away among the train carriages on the ferry for Turkmenbashi. (Dave Button)

I caught the same ferry that Dave would take two years later. Once that experience was over it was a drive of around 600km to the exhibition grounds.

'With this first part offloaded, I had a week to get to Almaty and back to Ashgabat to reload and clear the exhibition hall. It is around 4,000km as a round trip, including two borders each way. The representative for the exhibition was sweating buckets. He was adamant that I would never get back in time, but I assured him that I would and it would be fine, although he was still not convinced. The route I took was to Turkmenabat, and cross into Uzbekistan just beyond there. Onwards I went up to Tashkent, and slightly north to get to the border with Kazakhstan. Skirting the mountainous country of Kyrgyzstan on my right as such, it was a much flatter and easier drive. My delivery was to Almaty airport for a new shop development there. Customs was naturally close to the airport, which helped with the clearance for me to get the trailer empty. With that done I retraced my steps back. Having an empty trailer made the borders quicker, and I got back on the seventh day, perfectly in time to reload. Once again, I followed roughly the same route that I had just taken, back into Uzbekistan and then Kazakhstan. This time though I was heading for Moscow to offload this equipment and finally reload for home.'

Steve Tovey's journey there was taken overland, via Kazakhstan and Uzbekistan, no ferry crossing for him. He arrived at the Turkmenistan border on 17 March 1997.

'I remember the border between Uzbekistan and Turkmenistan being a pontoon bridge, which to put it politely was a bit past its prime. It moved side to side like a tree in a storm, and I really did wonder if I would get across without the whole lot ending up in the drink! I had someone directing me over, waving me on when the bridge had settled enough for me to make some progress. While on this border I met a duo of Kazakh drivers on their way to the same exhibition as me, driving a German-registered truck. They helped me exit Uzbekistan, which saved a fair bit of time. Then, as luck would have it, it was my turn to help. Upon entering the customs building on the Turkmen side, I handed my papers to a female customs agent. She saw my British passport and then proceeded to speak English far better than even I have! It turned out that she had been schooled at a private school in England before returning home. We were invited to have a cup of tea or three, and she soon had all our papers sorted and we were free to go. When I say free to go, there was one small issue. I did not have a visa. I paid the soldier on the gate to let me pass, which he did. Eventually, long after I had left someone must have caught onto the fact, and a warrant was issued for my arrest. En route a car was frantically trying to get me to stop on the side of the road. Knowing what sort of capers people pull once into the old Soviet countries there was no way I would stop for some car, and my Volvo soon outran his clapped out old Lada. When I was at the exhibition site at Ashgabat, the local police did manage to catch up with me. I had to go to the embassy there and arrange a visa, which took a few days, but I was eventually actually legally in the country.

'With the exhibition over, I was to head back to Moscow for the next show. I was asked to take a shorter, more direct route through Kazakhstan. This, however, would prove to be a very costly mistake. Heading north, around the area of Irgiz, the permafrost which is prevalent throughout the Steppe of Kazakhstan had begun to melt. This meant that I sank and got stuck; very, very stuck! To begin with I had raised the air all around to give myself maximum ground clearance, but when it got bogged down, it was down to the sump of the engine. When I shut the engine down to conserve diesel, the small air leaks that had amassed on the trip meant it sank on its haunches and that was that. Not far from me were two Finnish trucks going the other way who had the same problem, if not worse. We were pretty much in the middle of nowhere; there was a

Steve Tovey takes a break close to the town of Mary, en route to Ashgabat, Turkmenistan. (Steve Tovey)

small settlement nearby in some old railway carriages where a few people lived. When you get stuck like this, the only way out is the way you went in. A few trucks tried to help when they passed to get us out, but they had to carry on without any success. Even a 6 × 6 Kamaz tried in vain to help. One night, after getting back into my truck, I had left my boots outside as they were absolutely caked in mud. When I woke up, someone had stolen them, I could not believe it! I had literally seen no one for several days, yet at night someone had spirited my knackered mud-caked boots away!

'Two trucks from a large company called Central Asia Trans were heading

With the temperature warming, the ground was shedding itself of the ice … (Steve Tovey)

south. They stopped and tried but could not help. They then promptly got stuck not much further along. After nine days, two bulldozers managed to drag me out backwards, and I got going, only to get stuck further north! Another four days stuck in this spot and once again I was freed, this time for good. Having lost the best part of two weeks, not only was I keen to get going but so were Kepstowe. We had kept in touch via the satellite phone in the cab, and at one point they were looking at trying to get the army out to come and help me and the Finns out of our predicament. I managed to make the exhibition in Moscow by the skin of my teeth, much to everyone's relief.'

Left and below: Disaster for this Finn. With the permafrost melting, he has got stuck in a big way, as did Steve Tovey with him. (Steve Tovey)

Local trucks creating a daisy chain to help tow each other and a VW Passat from trouble. (Steve Tovey)

Back on solid ground, Steve's truck is white underneath that dirt. (Steve Tovey)

Uzbekistan

The fourth-largest CIS state, it is doubly landlocked, bordered by five landlocked countries. Uzbekistan was not one often visited, and when it was it was usually being transited.

Dave Button was sent to deliver a second-hand medical scanner trailer to Tashkent. It had been donated by a British charity for the people of Uzbekistan. His regular truck was a tag axle unit (a tag axle means the rear axle on the unit lifts), so it would not fit under this trailer as it was too long. Kepstowe had to rent a tractor unit from BRS for Dave to take. BRS kept hold of his regular unit as 'collateral' as they were so convinced he would not get it back to them!

'The route out was the usual tramp through Europe to the border at Smolensk, on to Moscow, and across to Chelyabinsk to the border close to Petropavl for Kazakhstan. Then it was a case of head towards Almaty. There is an alternative route, via the small town of Shu, that I tried to take. This cuts off a large corner of the route and avoids having to go near the capital. However, the police were not very keen on this. They stopped me and wanted to arrest me for attempting such a brazen act of driving down a perfectly good 'motorway'. In the end they settled for allowing me to sleep in the truck for the night at the police post, fining me in the morning but then allowing me to continue rather than turn me around. They were actually really nice about it, which made a bit of a change for the Russian police!

'With my pocket a little lighter, I continued to the town of Balkhash. Here the road runs alongside the huge lake named after the town. This stretch is akin to driving on corrugated iron, the ripples are horrendous. If they were bigger and deeper it would have been smoother, but they were not, so I just had a really uncomfortable drive, a little more so than usual. This also meant that the ailing trailer was suffering from this beating, and by the time I got to the capital the trailer was covered in ratchet straps to hold the various lockers and equipment in place. The next and last major town is Shymkent, and then to the border. When cleared, it is not far until you arrive in Tashkent. Once I found the delivery address, it was simply a case of drop the trailer where it was required, remove all of my straps and then the job was done. If only they could all be that simple to complete.

'Considering the road conditions, and the age of this scanner, it had fared quite well, and was still pretty much in working order when they tried it out. Now it was time to go home solo. This was give or take around 6,000km, with no trailer! There are two real options for routes back home. I could retrace my original route, or opt for a "short cut" across the steppe. Being as I was just in a tractor unit, I opted for the shorter route as I thought it would be easier and quicker. This was to be turning left at Shymkent and heading north towards Aralsk, then Aktobe before turning west for Uralsk and the border back into Russia, which would lead towards Samara. This would save me a good 1,500km or so. What I did not factor in was the ride quality. I know the roads can be rough, but driving across a virtual desert is really harsh. My bum spent more time in the air and my head hitting the truck's roof than me being sat as I would if I had been on an actual road. Some of the holes you could easily park a truck in, walk away and look back and you would not see it, they were huge. I was so glad to finally get back onto a Kazakh road near the border!

'As the unit was a rental, the office wanted me to get it back as quick as I could to save rental fees, so rather than collect a trailer in Moscow to take home I simply carried on overland. It also meant I could nip around the border queue and save myself a lot of time. When I got the truck back to BRS, they were rather surprised to see me, and handed me back my truck before taking this rental for a good jet wash and look over.'

Steve Tovey also visited the country a few times, taking computers and minting equipment to the Bank of Uzbekistan, located in the historic capital city of Tashkent. One trip did not quite go to plan, however.

Freelance driver Geoff Burton was providing some cover for Steve after selling his own truck. 'I had got as far as Nizhny Novgorod, and the clutch started playing up. Kepstowe told me to get it back to Moscow as there was a Volvo dealership there and none further east. I limped it back, and they flew me home. It was just before Christmas so that was an unexpected bonus, actually being home for the festive season. As it was Steve's truck I had been in, things were changed about so he would continue onwards with it when it was fixed.'

Steve recalls from here. 'Originally, I was due to take a MAN demonstrator truck to Moscow, but with my one breaking and the delays that created, that all changed. When we had loaded the computers for Tashkent, there were six loads in total. The job was for another haulier, Ralph Davis. As it ended up, me and Michael Mudie each had a load, two of Ralph's drivers, Vince Staunton and Bob Ervin. The last two had been loaded by Willi Betz, this was something that soon made it onto the rumour mill, people believing the work had gone for good! The Davis drivers had shipped out and spent Christmas and the New Year somewhere along the trail, whereas Michael's trucks had been shipped to Finland unaccompanied, so we spent Christmas and New Year at home before flying out and starting our run. On the way down Michael and myself were heading through Kazakhstan and were stopping at a truck stop nicknamed the Compulsory Shower. It was located somewhere before the town of Karaganda. When we pulled in, one of Ralph's trucks was in the parking area, although it turned out to be a chap called Mick Merell, who was on a separate job. Boy, was he pleased to see us! Being winter it was freezing cold, -10 or below, the ice made it difficult to stand up. He had been having some fuel issues after buying some at the roadside and had been towed here. He now had flat batteries; as most Russian trucks were still 12 volt, he was really struggling to get a jump start. We obliged and got the truck fired up for him, and finally he could start warming his truck up again. When we set off, he ran with us for a while to make sure it was all OK before he cracked on towards his destination of Almaty.

'As we carried on south, thankfully the weather grew steadily warmer, and the ice dissipated. We arrived in Tashkent about a week after Ralph's two drivers. They could not believe we had spent Christmas at home! All that was missing were the two Willi Betz trucks. As customs did not want to clear us without everyone being there, all we could do was wait. I cannot remember exactly how long we waited, but in the end, they cleared the four of us because the bank wanted to be getting as much installed as they could. There was still no sign of the Betz trucks, to this day I do not know when they arrived, but they must have taken a very scenic route to take so long. I know we had at least five days in the city.

'While we were there, Matt Towse had messaged us and asked if we could go and see a freight agent in town on their behalf about any reloads we could take on. Sadly, the only loads that he had were going to Islamabad. I was up for this as a bit of a challenge, but Matt was not so keen!' Steve recalls laughing. 'Once we were unloaded, Michael and I headed empty north back into the cold to Moscow to reload back to England.'

Kyrgyzstan

This country was barely touched by Kepstowe. Being so remote and impoverished, the basic infrastructure was lagging since the demise of the Soviet Union when it gained its independence.

A long journey's end. Steve Makin at the capital city of Kyrgyzstan, Bishkek. (Steve Makin)

To this day this situation has not greatly improved, the roads still leave a lot to be desired.

John Mantle and Steve Makin were the only Kepstowe drivers to venture to this remote country and theirs were possibly some of the first western trucks to deliver into Kyrgyzstan. They delivered loads on behalf of Kodak to Bishkek, the capital city, for its factory and offices recently opened there. 'It was such a beautiful country to visit,' John recalls. 'After the bleakness and mostly unchanging scenery of the central Asia steppe, it was like an oasis locked in by these big mountain ranges, absolutely stunning.'

Steve also visited while on the Kodak roadshow.

THE KODAK ROADSHOWS

Kodak, the global photography company, were a long-standing customer of Kepstowe. They would regularly deliver photographic paper on their behalf, mostly to Moscow and Kiev, but occasionally runs to further-flung cities would happen for the drivers. In 1997 Kodak decided to put on several roadshows to promote their company and products. The cavalcade would roll into a town, accompanied by a few crew members also travelling overland in a Winnebago. They would set up the show trailer in the town centre or point of interest. The first day would involve washing everything down and making it presentable before commencing the task of setting up all the equipment and show displays. Two days of public shows and giveaways were followed by a disco. It was similar in format to how the Radio One roadshows of the time were, with Kodak hoping they would prove as popular.

With all of this completed, it would take a day to dismantle, repack and hit the road again. Steve Makin did what could be argued as possibly the most varied trip of all for Kepstowe. The first of these roadshows that Steve did took him to Ukraine and Belarus. It wasn't just a case of the major or capital cities either. 'If you look on a map, if there is a largish town, pretty much we went there, including some that were not even marked.' The

The roadshow in full swing. (Dave Button)

Taking in the sights in Samarkand, Uzbekistan. (Steve Makin)

second roadshow was to take in some serious mileage. Covering most of the 'stans', as they are collectively known, of the east, the countries of Kyrgyzstan, Uzbekistan and so on, there was not much ground left uncovered. 'As long as a city, and I use the term city loosely, had a population of at least 10,000, we would do a show there. Kodak's plan was to swamp the market and beat their arch-rivals Fuji to the market share with compact affordable cameras,' Steve remembers.

The first stop on this ultra-long haul was to be Bishkek, the capital of Kyrgyzstan, then onto the city of Osh before exiting into Uzbekistan. 'The biggest problem with the passing of time and with so many small stops is I cannot remember every place we visited sadly. From Uzbekistan we went across into Kazakhstan and

Finally a straight, flat part of the road, time to celebrate. (Steve Makin)

Refuelling when and where you can, by any means. (Steve Makin)

Below and opposite: The 'road' between Bishkek and Osh. The Töö Ash Pass is only open for around four months of the year due to the weather. Even when it was open, traversing it was not exactly a walk in the park, as these photos show. (Steve Makin)

started working our way north through any town of note. The one country we did not visit down in that area was Tajikistan.'

Setting off from London at the end of March, this tour would take around five months to complete, ending back in Moscow at the start of September to coincide with the city's 850th celebrations, as covered elsewhere in this book.

Dave Button would also undertake one of these tours. His was around the Baltic states, which also included going into Russia's enclave of Kaliningrad. Dave recalls.

KEPSTOWE FREIGHT
VOLVO
F12
INTERCOOLER
GB
K4 KEP

Kodak

It was not all plain sailing. Due to the angle Steve had to wait until another truck came along to help tow him around the corner. (Steve Makin)

Right and opposite above: Dave Button's brightly liveried truck for the Kodak roadshow. Not easily missed on the roads! (Dave Button)

'I had just got home from another job when I was asked to take over this particular tour from another driver who had been taken ill. The next day I was on a flight out to Riga. After collecting the truck I headed to the coastal town of Liepāja, and from there we went south into Lithuania to Klaipėda. When this town's show had finished, we travelled south once again, heading for the Russian border, but not

how I usually knew it. This drive was on the Curonian Spit national park, just a small road through the trees. It was lovely. The border was really small, and I think they were surprised to see a truck turn up as this is not really any sort of route to anywhere that trucks would usually visit.

'Once the border formalities were complete, we headed to the town of Kaliningrad. It was a really pretty city to have a look around, quite different to most of the Russia I had seen before. When it was time to leave there, we headed east back into Lithuania and our next stop was Kaunas. Here things got a little hairy on the second day. As usual the roadshow had gone into disco mode, and everyone was having a dance. I was sat in my truck having a cup of tea, when I noticed there was a bit of a kerfuffle happening down the front of the stage. As with these sort of things, it soon escalated and more and more people were getting involved, which turned into pushing, into punching and even more people having a go. From out of nowhere, one of the men in the middle of it pulled a gun out and shot someone. Cue the pandemonium! Everyone scattered, leaving this one man on the floor bleeding but alive and certainly vocal about it unsurprisingly. An ambulance and the police arrived, took the injured man away and spoke with the local Kodak rep about what happened. Not quite the ending to the day I had expected.

'Thing is, at the time Kaunas had a bit of a reputation for being a bit like the Wild West, so in a way it was not surprising. The country had only recently become completely independent from Russia and so there, as well as the other Baltic states, a pecking order for honest and not so honest people was still sort of being ascertained. The next day we set off for Vilnius before venturing into Belarus and the capital, Minsk. From here I was flown home as I was purely providing some emergency cover and had not been home for the whole of May, so I needed some downtime. Michael Mudie was flown out to replace me and he continued on with Belarus and Ukraine.'

On the 'ferry' from Lithuania. Note the English-registered Winnebago, used by the Kodak crew as accommodation on the road. (Dave Button)

Incredibly, this was the official border between Lithuania and the Russian enclave of Kaliningrad. (Dave Button)

SOMETHING SLIGHTLY DIFFERENT ...

Not all Kepstowe work went east. Occasionally some of the touring work would take the drivers somewhere new. Lou Johnson found himself heading for the Balkans, territory outside the usual remit. For this job, he was at the helm of his usual steed, the company's Mercedes 814 rigid. This little truck was certainly unusual at the time, being left-hand drive and British registered. As with all the other trucks that Kepstowe had bought, it was of a very high specification, with not only the load's comfort in mind, but also the driver's. With optional extras such as an uprated alternator, luxury suspended driver's seat, reinforced front axle and springs, extra fuel tank and so on, it was a well-thought out truck. This had been bought to replace an older tilt-bodied Mercedes, which was subsequently sent to the Moscow depot to work internally.

Lou recalled: 'It was the year 2000 and I was on a theatre tour of the Shakespeare play, *The Tempest*, for the now defunct AandBC Theatre Company. Initially the itinerary was nothing too out of the ordinary. The cities went as follows: Canterbury, Prague, Brno, Gdansk, Edinburgh, London, Nizhny Novgorod, Samara, Saratov and Volgograd, Sibiu, Craiova and Bucharest. At some point during the undertaking of this tour, a few extra dates were added at the end. These were Tirana, Pristina, Kosovo and then Budapest. The only problem was that Kosovo had been in the deadly grasp of a civil war up until 1999. Although the war had officially ended, NATO/KFOR still had a very strong presence on the ground. There were still pockets of resistance within the city of Pristina.

'I remember when the job got added to, Rob Keir in the office spoke to me

Someone talented on the cast created a crew list on the tail lift of Lou's truck. (Lou Johnson)

Right and below: The streets of Pristina, showing the war damage and heavy military presence. (Lou Johnson)

on the phone about it, assuring me that as the war was over, there would be nothing to worry about. When I arrived in Pristina, I do not think everyone had received that memo! There was still plenty of firing going on all around, terrifying really. I remember when I managed to find a phone and call the office I said "Listen to this." Henry Osbourne replied: "Have you got thunder and lightning, it's really loud?" I wished I could have laughed at the time, instead I was somewhat direct in my answer to what the noises were!

'When the show here was over and my truck was loaded, I was certainly ready to head towards "safety". The route was south to Macedonia. It is around 50 miles to the border itself from the town. Of course, the queue heading that way was huge, nigh on 40 miles long. The road was rammed with trucks, cars and plenty of refugees still trying to flee. I joined the back of the queue and started to wait, thinking that I would be in for a long few days. After a couple of hours, a military Jeep pulled up alongside me. The general who was inside had been at the performance of the show in Pristina. He asked what the problem was. To be honest I could not believe he had not noticed the queue, so I pointed out this minor detail. Quick as a flash, he got in contact with the border post and got me permission to skip the queue, so off I went. I insisted he travelled with me; I knew what would happen if I went alone, I would have all sorts thrown at the truck. All of us Kepstowe drivers have witnessed this sort of thing with people chancing their arm at skipping the queue at other frontiers.

Locals' delight etched into Lou's dirty truck. (Lou Johnson)

'When I finally got to the front of the border, I was greeted by Russian military guards who were part of the UN force. With my experience of general Russian borders and their 'friendly and helpful' officials, I really thought it would take forever. Incredibly, one of the guards recognised the Kepstowe name as a regular in and out of his homeland. He personally sorted my paperwork immediately and away I went, probably the quickest I have ever been through a border with Russians involved. With all of that in the mirrors of the truck, as I entered Macedonia, I certainly breathed a big sigh of relief.'

THE END …

As the east continued to develop its infrastructure and shake off the last remnants of communism, it was more able to cope with haulage and logistics. As with most industries, the issue of price was a core reason for more work going to companies from the east. Kepstowe found it harder to compete and the work began to dwindle. One by one the sub-contractors found their work supply getting less, so found work elsewhere, much to their disappointment. With the lack of work, some of the full-time drivers had seen the writing on the wall and reluctantly handed their notice in, while a few remained for as long as they could. The decision was made in early 2003 to sell the remaining trucks and make the last drivers redundant. Not an easy decision but Kepstowe had few other options. They carried on trading as a freight forwarder. With so much more competition, especially from countries that could offer a much cheaper alternative now everything had opened up, at the end of 2004 the company ceased trading.

Fleetwood/Richard Warren

Richard's final trip to Russia sadly ended in disaster, shortly after crossing the border with Chris Everitt into Russia at Smolensk on Wednesday, 8 July 1998.

'There was a police post near to the Smolensk Motel. I had just passed it heading up the hill. A Russian Maz truck pulling an empty, German-owned tilt trailer was coming the other way. He was catching up some slower-moving traffic but did not want to pull out to overtake as it was so close to the police post. As we got almost level he braked, which caused him to jackknife. With literally nowhere to go, I slammed headfirst into his thankfully empty trailer. It was caused because his truck and trailer were not compatible. He could not connect all the air lines up, so he had no brakes working on the trailer.'

The impact initially knocked Richard out cold. He was cut from head to toe, and in a bad way. Trapped in the seat by the steering column, Chris managed to free him from the cab with the help of some other Russian drivers.

'I remember I kept saying to Chris don't let them cut my legs off. It is all still a bit hazy. They managed to get an ambulance and I was taken off to the nearest hospital. I was covered not only in cuts, but also antifreeze, power steering fluid and small shards of glass. I was black and blue all over with bruises, but I also remember that when they got me to the hospital, the table they laid me onto was especially uncomfortable! At no point was I cleaned up, so all the vehicle fluids, glass and so on stayed with me for the duration. The doctor proceeded to stitch some of the cuts up on my head while I lay in agony on this damned table. It felt like the needle was coming out the other side of my head, it was horrific. It turned out afterwards that they had laid me on a post-mortem examination table! The hospital was not exactly what you would call clean; the toilet you could find in the dark by following your nose. If you wanted to wash you had to turn the tap on for a few minutes and run the tea-coloured water out of the system first, it was a right mess! The nurses were not really trained to be nurses either, so when it came to injection time, it was always a challenge for them to find a vein and administer the drugs successfully.'

After a couple of days, Chris, along with Mickey Packham, who had been diverted to come and assist, bribed the head doctor to discharge Richard early so he could be sent for some proper medical attention.

'Fortunately, my insurance through Transmed covered the lot, including my

Above, left and overleaf: The horrific aftermath of Richard Warren's crash at Smolensk. With Richard in hospital, Alan collected the wreck to transport it back to the UK. (Alan Johnson & Mickey Packham)

SCANIA
GB

repatriation. I was taken to the Smolensk Motel, where all I could do was lay on the bed and wait. Initially, Transmed were going to send an ambulance from Moscow to collect me and take me back there. However, they could not arrange an ambulance for over a week, so they managed to get me into the passenger seat of Chris Everitt's truck and he took me to Moscow.'

He was dropped off at the Holiday Inn Hotel at Sheremetyevo airport. 'A lot of it is still a haze. However, I remember being in the hotel room the night before the flight, thinking to myself I really should at least try and have a wash before the flight. I was still in the same clothes as the crash. But as it had been several days now, the fluids as well as my blood had congealed and dried all around the waistband of my trousers along with any body hair, and after one or two attempts at removing them, the agony of it nearly knocked me out, so I gave that idea up.'

Richard flew back to the UK. Upon landing though there was another problem. He physically could not get out of the plane seat as his legs had seized solid in the seat. No one back home had really been told the extent of his injuries, it should have been a full medical evacuation. Nobody had informed the airline either, who were somewhat disgruntled with Richard, somewhat unfairly as he had merely been handed a plane ticket and told to board the flight.

Visiting his local doctor, he could not believe the Russian's handiwork with the stitching and 'care', and was promptly sent to hospital, where it emerged that both of his kneecaps were broken. 'How I managed to get about at all with both of them like that I have no idea to this day!' He ended up in plaster for six months.

The Scania itself was left at the Intourist Hotel at Smolensk. The trailer he was pulling was not too badly damaged, so it was promptly collected, and the load was delivered. The insurance company, to everyone's amazement, wanted the truck recovered and returned for repair rather than written off. Alan Johnson had just delivered to Ganja, Azerbaijan, and was tasked with bringing it back home.

'I had heard on the grapevine about Richard's crash, but when I saw the truck it sent a shiver down my spine,' recalls Alan.

'One of the biggest problems with the wreck was the width. Because the cab was so twisted it was a lot wider than a "normal" truck, so we had to obtain oversize permits to take it back. In the end the routing changed completely due to this, and I ended up taking it back to Finland and shipping directly back to the UK. In all honesty I have no idea why the insurance company wanted it back, there really was not much you could salvage from it.'

When the insurance company realised that the truck was a write-off, they promptly paid out for the loss. Richard then purchased a second-hand Volvo F16 Globetrotter, which at the time was a top of the range flagship vehicle. Nick Reynolds sold his share of the company to Richard and emigrated to America, where he still resides. Richard continued doing some long-distance work, initially to Morocco for John Mann Transport. His fleet grew slowly but surely, taking in several former Kepstowe drivers. With the ever-evolving world of transport, the fleet was trimmed, and now Richard operates just the one truck, still on international transport. He still owns the F16, which is now in preservation.

'About two trips previous to my final one, I believed the writing was on the wall for us running east. I had seen over a dozen brand new, Superspace-cabbed DAF trucks coupled to brand new tilt trailers bought in Holland, all heading east to be registered and start work. Up until that point, most of the Russian trucks were dilapidated wrecks that could not go to Western Europe. As it opened up and money was invested, the trucks got newer and they were able to compete, and quickly become far cheaper than British haulage.'

Alan King and Alan Douglas went on to sub-contract for a company called PSL, based in Maldon, Essex. They specialised in transport to Iberia, with the pair finding the much more clement weather far nicer to work in. The lack of border queues was certainly a bonus, both drivers heartily agreed.

Alan Johnson's last trip to Russia was in August 1999, delivering to Moscow and reloading house removals back to the UK. While the Russian work had ended for him, an exhibition in Barcelona afterwards provided a much easier trip, along with the Edinburgh festival requiring some logistics in 2000. 'After that work became scarce, I found work for several other people. I ended up having a couple of Kepstowe's old tractor units, which I put to work but not on the routes east any more.' Alan is now semi-retired, offering the occasional abnormal load escort service in his van.

Dave Button made his final trip in September 2001. 'I took exhibition equipment to Warsaw in Poland for a medical convention. When I returned I knew the best was gone so I handed my notice in and finished this great chapter in my life. From memory only Pete Newlyn and Michael Mudie were left at that point, mostly moving containers and undertaking local work only.'

EPILOGUE

The Russian runs that were undertaken were not as well documented at the time compared to other golden times of transport. Several other companies did also capitalise on the lucrative money offered for the work. As with most lines of transport, some were more successful than others, often with the ones trying to do it cheaply finding it cost them more in the long run. As we have seen, the mosaic of road haulage is a constantly shifting one and at the time of writing, Russia has invaded Ukraine. The opportunity for any road haulage across this area is even more limited and difficult. I am glad I got to dip my toe into this world with some of my own work. Nothing as challenging or pioneering as the drivers in this book, and I would love the opportunity one day to do more. It was a pleasure to share such great memories while researching this book, even the ones that the drivers are glad are now distant memories, from this interesting part of transport history.